FRIENDS FACE REALITY

FRIENDS
FACE REALITY

by

HAROLD LOUKES M.A.
READER IN EDUCATION, UNIVERSITY OF OXFORD

THE BANNISDALE PRESS
LONDON

First Published 1954
Reprinted 1956
Reprinted (with revisions) 1961

Copyright 1954 by The Bannisdale Press
46-47, Chancery Lane, London. W.C.2

Printed in Great Britain by
Charles Birchall and Sons Ltd.,
Liverpool and London

ACKNOWLEDGMENTS

Acknowledgments are due to the following for their permission to quote from copyright sources: John Farquharson on behalf of the Estate of the late William James; George Allen & Unwin Ltd. for quotations from Roger Wilson's *Authority, Leadership and Concern*, and Howard Brinton's *Friends for 300 Years;* the Oxford University Press for The *Poems* of Francis Thompson, Bertrand Russell's *Religion* and *Science*, Nisbet and Co. Ltd. for *The Relevance of Christianity*, Penguin Books for Bowlby's *Child Care and the Growth of Love* and Dr. Carpenter's *Christianity*, the Bannisdale Press for *Quaker Worship* and the Friends' Intelligencer for the article on a meeting for worship; and to the Friends' Literature Committee, and the Friends' World Committee for Consultation.

List of Contents

CHAPTER ONE

Retreat from Religion

WHEN a thinking man finds himself face to face with the question, 'What am I here for?' where does he look for an answer?

At one time he would have turned to the church, for there he would have found other thinking men exploring the problem with a mixture of knowledge and hope, discovery and search, and certitude and honest doubt, that would at least have reassured him by claiming that his question was important, and an answer could be sought for. Until a generation or so ago, that would have been the obvious thing to do. It is what men would have expected of a sensible enquirer. When he did it, he would have found many points of doubt, many subjects of dispute; but he would have been impressed by a certain air of authority and conviction, of acceptance of the Christian framework, not merely the external authority to which sections of the church laid claim, but the inward authority that springs from honest and exhaustive and comprehensive thought.

Those days are gone, and the authority of the church has gone too. We know where to go for guidance about our bodies or our mental processes, our economic life or our æsthetic achievement. These things have their experts – and though experts are wrong sometimes, they have their standing, and we treat them seriously. But on the fundamental question – surely the most fundamental of all questions – What are we here for? there is now no one to speak with more authority than another. The leader-writer, thumping his typewriter at midnight, is sure of a wider audience than an archbishop preparing his Christmas message. Where then do we turn, if not for an answer, at least for help in seeking our own answer, to this basic problem of the nature of our being and destiny?

There are those to say it does not matter. We cannot know, they argue, and like helpless drifters in an oarless boat we must leave our ends to be determined by the tide, imperceptible and

9

uncontrollable. It is easier to accept this counsel at some periods than at others: to eat and drink and wait for the death that comes tomorrow. It is easy to do that when food and drink are plentiful, and good companions fill our lives with fun. But at other times things do not go so well: instead of food and drink there is famine; and our good companions fall to an enemy shell. It is in such a period that we live today, a period in which we are not contented enough to banish the question, too profoundly disturbed not to ask where the tide is carrying us, and wondering too whether we are so helpless after all. The question presses upon us with an urgency almost unrivalled in the past; and yet – and here is the grim irony of it all – and yet the recognized authorities for answering ultimate questions have lost their prestige at precisely the moment when we need them most.

Thinking men would believe almost any other authority more easily than the church. They would not take much account, perhaps, of the 'views of the famous film star' which appear in the newspapers; but the views of a physicist on the spiritual significance of man, or of a psychologist on the possibility of an after-life, or of a chemist on the moral aspect of modern war – these are canvassed freely, and receive a publicity which the innocent scientist himself frequently deplores.

Why is this? A sensible man would naturally turn to the medical profession with its hospitals if he were in search of health; if he sought learning, he would turn to scholars, with their colleges and universities. Why should he not inevitably turn to the bishops and clergy, with their churches, for answers to his final questions? To the enquirer, it would seem odd that we should ask this question at all. The answer is obvious, he would reply. The churches are not concerned with the questions I want to ask. They are irrelevant to the issue. They are out of date, out of date themselves and out of date in their thought. They would seek to answer my questions with a story taken from history, two thousand years old. And more recent history would be pressed in to explain why different groups of churchmen give different answers, even to the length of telling different versions of the original story on which it is all based. I want something modern: I am modern; my problems are modern and urgent; and I want an answer that looks at them fairly and takes account of the context in which they arise. 'They have an impression', says Dr. Carpenter in his recent book, *Christianity*, referring to these same sensible enquirers, 'that it has ceased to be relevant. A view commonly encountered at Padre's Hours, during the War, was, "That is quite interesting, and very likely true. But it all happened a long time ago, and I want something more contemporary, or as some put it, less static." ' Churchmen have recognized the force of this demand by the extent to which they have sought to answer it.* And it would now be widely admitted that the achievements of Christianity in the past are not for most men a reason for paying much attention to it in the present, apart from the obvious value of understanding our origins, with all the enlightenment and breadth and tolerance that that may give.** But what matters is the 'weight' the church carries now, the power it can bring to bear on problems of present conduct, the explanation it can give of knowledge and ignorance in their twentieth century form. 'Can Christianity come out in the open,' asks one of the same bishops that the enquirer would prefer not to consult, 'take a survey of the various new factors, psychological, economic, sociological, and offer creative moral leadership at once more progressive and more stable than non-Christian thinking can promise?' These words were written in 1931; but though the need for this creative thinking is more urgent than ever in the dark that has fallen on us since, the non-Christian would still feel that the Church had not risen to its own vision of its task.

A special aspect of this 'irrelevance' is the extent to which past divisions are perpetuated in an apparently frozen continuity of sectarianism. There may be movements towards unity of which churchmen are hopefully aware, but viewed from outside, Christian organization is marred by divisions that, even when they arose, were unpardonable, and are now ridiculous. If a sensible enquirer were to be drawn towards a vague, indeterminate, hesitantly Christian interpretation of life, he would find his first steps barred by the demand to assume a definite, confident, even arrogant judgement on issues which he had no hope of ever solving, and no particular desire to solve. Anxious, shall we say, to find grounds for his hope that the Christian view of man is the true one, he would be asked to decide first whether there were seven sacraments or two, or whether the modern bishop was in a line of continuous physical contact with Saint Peter, or to

*e.g. F. R. Barry, *The Relevance of Christianity*; Dean Inge, *The Christian Ethic and Modern Problems*.
**See Livingstone: *Education and the Spirit of the Age.*

choose between several conflicting views of the spiritual, economic and functional status of the clergyman. Some of these questions he could not avoid. The churchman, 'inside', is able to avoid them because he has grown up in one tradition, and can accept it as being as good as any other. But the enquirer has to decide, in plain terms, 'where he will go to'. There is, for him, no such thing as 'the Church', an ideal concept which the believer can cherish to comfort himself against the oddities of different churches. For the enquirer there are only these same different churches: and he must make his mind up about which he will go to. Sectarianism, it must be admitted, renders the Christian gospel less relevant to the present situation than it ought to be.

Another factor in the situation is the way irrelevance begets irrelevance. If a doctor is not called upon by the sick, his knowledge will rust and his prestige decline, and he will lose even the patients he had. And as the church has declined in prestige, its numbers have declined, until the very size of the membership is a warning to an enquirer that his answer is unlikely to be here. Compare the empty church with the full cinema or the packed concert hall; the small, irregularly attended, Bible class with the large, flourishing classes in art or scraper-board or popular economics, philosophy, psychology and all the rest in the multitudes of evening classes; and there is visible another reason for the enquirer's refusal to 'go to church'. 'What men despise is despicable': this is not true, but it has truth enough to be one of the vital principles of modern advertising; and modern advertising is made to 'work'. The decline of the churches has left a vacuum which other forces have hastened to fill: mass entertainment, for those who would forget the problems and enjoy the life they no longer hope to explain; adult education, for those who would know at least what there is to be known. And active in inspiring these two sets of institutions, the artists and intellectuals, scientists and technicians who have seized the glories and the pride of place. The old, open war between 'science' and 'religion' is over; but only because 'science' has conquered virtually all the territory to which it laid claim, and 'religion' has withdrawn from the field where the engagement took place. In a sense, 'science' has won, and we are all scientists now. The struggle has left its legacy, and it is widely assumed that because 'science' has won, 'religion' has lost; and though 'science' may not be able to tell us everything, 'religion' can tell us nothing. These are the tacit assumptions in most minds, though they are not dragged out into the open, because the old conflict between science and religion is now seen to have been a false issue from the start. But there is, even now, a concealed conflict, a tendency towards divergence, in which 'science' is winning, unintentionally, fields to which it has never seriously laid claim. And because of that, the enquiring mind is diverted from organized religion into other, freer, more modern and attractive roads.

For he cannot escape the suspicion – and here we come to what is perhaps at the heart of the modern aversion from the church – that if a man were to seek the truth about life from organized Christianity, he would be met by closed minds, who would offer him established prejudices, messages handed on from the past, and dogmas that paid no attention to the changed conditions of life in a century which seemed to offer change as almost the only unchanging thing. When Paul met the philosophers at Athens, he said,* 'As I passed by, and beheld your devotions, I found an altar with this inscription, TO THE UNKNOWN GOD. Whom therefore ye ignorantly worship, him declare I unto you.' Now there are good reasons why Paul should talk like this, but it must surely be confessed that the philosophers would find it irksome. The spirit of enquiry is the search for 'the unknown God'; and if someone were in honesty and humility of mind to be searching for a truth he had not found, he would shrink from a situation in which he was likely to be accused of superstition because he had not found it. (The philosophers in Athens, of course, deserved all they got. They had already called Paul a 'babbler', and a 'setter forth of strange gods'; and they spent their time 'in nothing else, but either to tell, or to hear some new thing'. If their interest in Paul's cataclysmic experience was merely idle curiosity, then Paul was right to deal sharply with them; but the fact remains that the genuine, honest enquirer could be deterred from enquiring of a Christian because of this note of certainty, the tendency to claim that doubts are settled once and for all, and that a state of enquiry is somehow rather unsatisfactory – as it is, perhaps at the end of a search, but not at the beginning.)

The Christian gives the impression of being 'committed' to a prepared position, as having declared himself, as having closed his mind to certain questions. And so, of course, he must when

*Acts 17, 23.

he has made a degree of progress in understanding, as a mathematician no longer has an open mind about a geometrical proof. But while the mathematician can demonstrate to others what is now beyond argument to himself, the Christian has no easy method of demonstration – and yet sounds, so often, more convinced than would seem reasonable to his listener. *Dogmatic* – the very etymology of the word carries its own implication: the dogma of Christianity has a settled, predetermined appearance which makes it unapproachable to the hesitant seeker who asks that we should sit and reason together.

The conflict is not as modern as it may be made to look: men have argued the claims of Reason and Faith before today; but it has become more acute in modern times because 'reason' has achieved such spectacular success. Theoretical science has turned itself into applied science, and produced shining, mysterious instruments of impressive complexity and power. Faith has nothing comparable to show. In the circumstances, organized religion cannot but seem irrelevant, dowdy, feeble, tattered, slightly pathetic, to the man who looks out honestly and judges what he sees.

And yet this sad remnant still make their claims, and the honest seeker is still, despite all these things, unable to ignore them. Handicapped as they are, the Christian sects still hold that they are trustees of an experience which honest seekers after truth must reckon with. Of their handicaps they are usually more bitterly aware than the detached observer. They know that historic events have forced on them divisions which they would heal if they could. They know they have declined in numbers and prestige, and that an orthodox Christian point of view is less acceptable outside the church than an unorthodox one, and that a doctor would be expected to have sounder views on marriage than a priest. And above all they know, for they feel it in their own pulses, the present tension between 'reason' and 'faith', science and dogma.

This book is an attempt to present the sort of answer to these problems which a particular section of the church has found. It must be the answer of a single sect, because in this tragic situation that is the only answer that could be real. Despite the fact that its roots are in the past, Christianity has always been expressed in the living present, in dynamic corporate life, and standards of behaviour that met the dangers of the age; and in our present this living Christianity is practised in the sects. It is *less* than Christianity, but it is the only sort there is. It would be futile to attempt to state the essential tenets of Christianity in a form acceptable to all Christians, and to publish it and say, Here is the Christian answer! That would be the true irrelevance. Even as an intellectual statement it would look very thin, with all the controversial elements shorn away, for it is always the vital elements that are controversial. But more than this, it would be irrelevant because it would not be the reality of the Christian experience. Christianity involves action, and action is performed by people and groups of people. 'God is love' – what does this mean without the illustration of loving deeds? Set down in cold print, elaborated in argument, passionately uttered in words – how pale and ineffective it sounds compared with the kiss that St. Francis set on the lazar's lips! And it will, if it is true Christianity that is to be described, need the expression of action in groups. The Christian experience is something that happens to people in community: the disciples, Pentecost, the monastery, the congregation, the meeting for worship. It does, indeed, enrich the life of the individual, and some great, lonely souls have sought this enrichment to the detriment of their fellowship with others, but the *characteristic* Christian experience is one of communion with God in a heightened awareness of our dependence upon each other.

The Christian cannot answer the charge of irrelevance to the need of the day, therefore, without describing the work of this impulse to fellowship; and it must be a real fellowship, a specific group, composed of men and women, old and young, wise and foolish, and not merely of Man in his social aspect. 'Life in our town' is best described, not by a list of civic functions or splendid entertainments, but by the daily trivialities of 'Life in our street'; and the Christian life is best described in terms of the life of Christians. So the man who asks where Christianity is to be found, must be answered out of the sects whose very existence is a scandal to him. He must draw what comfort he can from the fact that to the sectarians themselves it is a scandal deeper and more tragic.

There is a special ironic twist in the fact that the sect I am going to describe is, as it were, a sect against sectarianism. At the time of its origin, in the seventeenth century, schism and separatism were in the air, and Christians were fiercely divided about matters that some thought of little importance. The peculiarity of the early Quakers was their claim that what men were divided about did not matter, that the argument was all directed in the wrong direction, and that if men would seek honestly, they would find the truth, unaided by all the elaborate systems of belief and ritual which other sects were arguing about. It was a movement, this early Quakerism, that never sought to be a sect; that sought to put an end to all sects. But the climate of the time was against it, and despite itself (as other powerful movements have had to do) it became a sect. And there it is today, one like the rest, conscious of its loss in its isolation; conscious of the loss to the whole Christian community and to the effectiveness of the Christian witness that springs from the divisions, and yet still unable to see a way to heal them. It is a long journey to retread the mistaken paths of history, and they can never be simply forgotten. Animosities and irritations *may* be forgotten – and humbly and thankfully we may claim that these at least are beginning to disappear. But the divisions arose because different men felt it necessary to lay different emphases on aspects of the truth. If the whole truth is a complex thing (and is it not?) made up of something scattered through these different, and often conflicting, accounts, then the sects would do no service to the truth by lightly abandoning their positions. It is in honesty that they hold on.

Quakers have a peculiar responsibility in this situation, for they have parted company from all other sects by reason of their very claim that the whole doctrinal and ritualistic argument of the seventeenth century was irrelevant. As the Rev. Oliver Tomkins said, in bringing greeting from the World Council of Churches to the world conference of Friends at Oxford in 1952,

> You are in many ways a standing perplexity to most of us. You have decided to dispense, at least in the form in which they are received amongst most of us, with certain ordinances which we believe to be God's expressed will for His people. However much other Christians differ for example over Baptism, the Lord's Supper and on a separated ministry, they agree in accepting what you do without. Yet you steadily show the fruit of the spirit in a way which continually makes us ask in what sense these things are necessary to life in Christ.*

That is precisely the function that Friends feel themselves driven to assume: to be a standing perplexity, and to make

*Friends Face their Fourth Century, p.7.

Christians ask in what sense the things they value are necessary to life in Christ. They feel these questions need to be asked, though as long as they must stand in isolation to ask them, they themselves suffer as much as any from the division. They are the poorer for their obstinacy, yet cannot but be obstinate.

That is why this book appears to discuss, if you like, the 'relevance of Quakerism'. It is a small and unpretentious sect, with its most vigorous life, to all appearances, in the past, and its achievements in some ways unimpressive. But to the enquirer who wishes to know what Christianity is before he either rejects it or pursues it further, Quakerism holds a certain weight of truth which demands attention. Its central emphasis may be said, indeed, to be laid on the importance of enquiry itself; for in an age when men were divided as to the external authority for their belief, the Quakers stood out for attention to an internal authority. When they debated the rival claims of church and book, Quakers urged the claim of a voice within the human heart.

It was no accident that modern science and Quakerism were born together, for they represent the spirit of enquiry at work in the fields of physical and spiritual reality. As the scientist set out to know the physical world for himself, so the early Quaker set out with the belief that man could know the spiritual world for himself, without intervention from priest or presbyter. And so this book sets out to tell, as far as cold print can tell, something of what they have found by the way.

CHAPTER TWO

The Effect of Science

THE scientist, I have said, was determined to see the physical world for himself. This determination has now become so much an assumption that it is difficult to re-capture the mental attitudes of the time before it was possible. But the medieval scientist approached his studies from a very different point of view. Instead of turning, open minded and without prejudice, to the study of 'what is', he was almost wholly preoccupied with 'what ought to be'. Even his experiment was largely directed to the search of what ought to exist, such as the philosopher's stone, rather than to the scrutiny of what did exist. In his search, he found out a good deal about what did exist, but that was accidental and unintentional, and rarely organized in such a way as to be useful for further study.

An illustrative contrast between the two modes of thought is provided by Galileo's work on acceleration. The middle ages believed that the acceleration of a falling body was in proportion to its weight: that a pound of lead would fall twice as fast as half a pound, and half as fast as two pounds. This assumption was unchallenged because it was a matter of reason, of *a priori* argument. It was true because it 'ought' to be. Galileo, approach-ing the problem in the manner we now regard as the natural one, decided to drop different weights to see if it were really so. He therefore climbed the leaning tower of Pisa and performed his experiments; only to prove that the general assumption was wrong, and that larger and smaller weights reached the ground together. This, says Bertrand Russell, 'proved to Galileo that Aristotle was wrong, but to the other professors that Galileo was wicked.'*

'Aristotle was wrong', because Aristotle's mixture of observ-ation and untested reasoning provided the authoritative account of the physical world, which the medieval mind never expected to overturn. It was a wonderful account, remarkable in its

*In *Religion and Science.*

completeness and unity, and in the way all known facts were bound together in a system which applied to the whole of human life. What we should now divide into astronomy, mathematics, physics, geology, chemistry, psychology, physiology, theology, philosophy and the rest was united in an inter-related system of knowledge and conventional ignorance which could not be tinkered with. It stood or fell together, and one who tried, as Galileo tried, to emend a part was laying profane hands on a sacred fabric. A brief account of some of the main ideas will make this clear.

The universe was created from the four elements, earth, fire, air and water; which were in turn created from four contrary 'properties', hot, cold, wet, dry, which were the constituents of chaos. Thus, hot and dry would produce fire; hot and moist, air; cold and moist, water; and cold and dry, earth. These sorted themselves into place by natural 'desires', earth, the heaviest and most impure, seeking the centre of the universe; water next to it, air next, and fire flying out towards the circumference, where it concentrated into the stars and planets. The purest fire was that of the fixed stars, which were set in a vast globe, outside the spheres in which the seven planets moved at their respective distances from the earth. Outside the fixed stars was another sphere, the *primum mobile*, by which motion was transmitted to the other spheres by God, who was himself outside the *primum mobile*, and worked upon it by love. The universe might thus be regarded as a gap in the divine substance, a spherical area of imperfection within the perfect, upon which God worked to achieve his own perfection.

The manner of his working was inseparably connected with what had been observed of the behaviour of the stars and planets. The Spirit worked through matter to reach the spirit of man.

> On man heavens influence workes not so,
>   But that it first imprints the ayre,
> Soe soule into the soule may flow,
>   Though it to body first repaire,

as Donne sang, defending his elevation of profane love by an appeal to the working of divine love. The business of astrology was the study of the manner in which the sky thus worked on human character and destiny. It was a complex influence, for the planets interfered with each other; and a horoscope was thus a highly technical thing. The influence of the planets rose and fell as the hours passed, for each had an hour, succeeding to another until seven hours later when its turn came again. The days of the week were connected with the planets too, and the first, eighth, fifteenth and twenty-second hours of its own day were the hours of its greatest influence. On Sunday the sun worked for good fortune, inspiring with wisdom and liberality those who were born under its influence. Then the moon, with its wandering disposition, caused men's wits to wander, and caused lunacy, corruption and decay. Tuesday is so called after the Norse god Tiw, a rough equivalent of Mars, whose day it was, and who brought the good and ill of war, courage and cruelty, triumph and disaster. And so through the week these influences continued, leaving to this day their legacy in our words and idioms: saturnine, jovial, martial, venereal, mercurial, lunatic; and the very word 'disaster' itself, speaking of a catastrophic interference of the stars with the plans of man.

At the same time, the affairs of men were affected in another way by physical causes, for human character was based on the same four 'contraries' that went to the elements of the physical world. Now they were combined to form the four 'humours', hot and dry producing choler; hot and moist, blood, the sanguine humour; cold and dry, melancholy; cold and moist, phlegm. These too have left their influence on our vocabulary, but the weight of meaning carried in the middle ages has largely gone. 'Choleric' is but a faint shadow of the character that tended towards changeableness and vindictiveness, was indicated by a long, thin spare body and a saffron face, and made its subject apt to dream of fire and thunder and brightly coloured dangers. 'Sanguine' similarly meant plump and 'comfortable', with a pure red and white face, a good sleeper dreaming of 'bloody things or things pleasant', peppery in temper but not vindictive. The phlegmatic man was fat, pale and sleepy, dreaming of things watery or of fish, slow and dull in learning, and timid and fearful in spirit; while the melancholy man was the typical scholar, lean and spare in build, yellow in face, sleeping badly and suffering alarming dreams when he did, obstinate ('stiffe in opinions'), timorous and angry and sulky. Each man would be affected by all these humours, but the general tendency of his character would be determined by the humour which was in the greatest excess in his disposition; and the word 'complexion' was used to indicate the proportions of the four humours, with the characteristic tendency to which they gave rise.

With this, even more than with the theories of the planets and stars, there was mixed a great deal of shrewd observation; and indeed a modern psychologist has remarked that the medieval system still stands as the nearest approach to a workable classification of character types. There can be discerned a certain rough correspondence between the physical manifestations and temperamental qualities which the doctrine of the humours linked together.

It is not to be wondered at, then, that the system, which thus embraced the study of man as well as the study of the universe, should seem to stand four-square against an attack on any part of it and why Galileo's discoveries seemed so shocking and so dangerous. If a thing seems to be so, and can also be demonstrated as necessary in logic, it is disturbing to discover that it is not so after all. When to this natural tendency is added the effect of reverence, the habit of mind developed by steady attention to the wonders of the physical world as a sign of the greatness of God; and, again, the connexion between a settled order of belief and a settled order of society; and, again, more lamentably but equally understandably, the fact that the leaders of the church felt their own power and prestige to be implicated in this solid system of knowledge, belief, morality and organization, so closely interwoven together; when all this is considered, there can be no surprise that a scientist who came along looking with his own eyes was regarded as a dangerous nuisance. The church had a monopoly of knowledge, for only inside the organization of the church, as a priest or monk or minor clerk, could one become learned at all. And a monopoly of learning is subject to the laws that govern all monopolies: the first attack on the outworks, the first attempt to seize a part of the monopolized territory for another power, is resisted with all the resources the occupying force can mobilize.

It was thus with Copernicus and Galileo and the other early explorers of the truth. The Dominicans trained in dialectic, the Inquisition with weapons less subtle but more cruel, were all called on to defend the citadel. But they were defeated, as they had to be, until by the seventeenth century that particular struggle was over. 'Science' had won the right to make use of first hand observation against authority, and had in the process changed a complete method of thought. Learning could now begin in observation instead of authority and exposition: a lecturer could now tell what he had found, instead of expounding what he had been told.

This change in method, from logic and deduction to observation and induction, was decisive and not to be reversed, but it was not made at once applicable to the whole field of human experience. It applied to the macrocosm but not to the microcosm, to astronomy but not humanity; and 'religion', as a human phenomenon, remained unaffected. There were contemporary movements within the religious field which bore a rough correspondence with the movement of scientific thought, and were dealt with by the Inquisition in much the same way; but they were not for the moment based on the same presuppositions, nor did they work in the same manner. Science had conquered a territory, but it had not stormed the citadel; and for a time there remained a division of authority which left both religion and science masters in their own domain. The Newtonian physics, developed in the direct line of descent from Galileo and Copernicus, offered no challenge to religion, but accepted the idea of God as the Great Mechanic, who wound up the universe and then withdrew, leaving it to run by its own laws. There was now no room for belief in an arbitrary interference in human affairs through the instrument of the stars; nor, as the withering of the belief in witchcraft was to show, through tempest and external nature; but there was no direct attack on the Hebrew account of Creation or the general concept of a universe planned to the last detail as a school for man's obedience.

The attack on this central concept was to come in the nineteenth century, when the geologist and biologist combined to present a body of unsettling evidence about the date and method of creation. The accepted date was that proposed by Archbishop Ussher, 4004 B.C., some time in October, and with the six specific stages assigned to particular days of the week, so that it was known that man was created on a Friday. This story was first challenged by the geologists, by the publication of Hutton's *Theory of the Earth*, which set out the concept of geological time as we are now familiar with it, producing the evidence of the rocks and fossils to show that the earth must be indescribably older than Archbishop Ussher would have allowed. The book appeared in 1788, which was no time for a popular welcome, even from secular men, to any revolutionary doctrines. It was to be many years before ordinary British opinion could face any thought of reform, for the thought of reform was to be linked, almost immediately after the book appeared, with the rolling heads of the *Place de la Guillotine*.

The storm did not break, therefore, until the biologists, working some years later, presented their challenge, in a form at once more shocking and inescapable than that of the geologists. The story of Genesis implied that God had created the animals in the form we were now familiar with; had handed them over to Adam to be named; and had then left them alone. Against this was set evidence which proved that animals we no longer knew had once been common, and that the animals we still saw had not always existed in precisely their present shape. The species had not always been unchanged, and instead of creation in six days, we must substitute the conception of evolution over millions of years. Furthermore, man was himself a part of the whole process, and instead of tracing his ancestry to a special creation on a particular Friday in 4004 B.C., he must look further back to an origin which he shared with the monkeys and apes still swinging in the jungle.

At first it seemed as if the new conflict was to be a struggle to the death of one belief or the other. Evolution seemed to make nonsense of the doctrine of the Fall, and therefore to destroy its positive counterpart, the hope of Redemption, and thus to take away the central significance of the work of Christ, and the church he had called into being. A long and sometimes bitter struggle delayed its own conclusion by aligning the disputants into 'parties' and thus making an honest approach to the truth harder than it might have been. There is nothing to be gained from raking over the embers of this dead controversy, for the argument itself is over; but its effects remain in odd corners, and there are still many who believe, joyfully or reluctantly according to their bent, that the issue is still open. I have heard Christians say that evolution 'is all a lot of rubbish'; and there are others who still think that to be up to date one must believe that Christianity is 'unscientific'.

But for all that, this particular debate is concluded, and the position of the scientist has been largely conceded. We are all scientists now, for we all adopt the scientific method when dealing with certain fields of knowledge; and we should none of us now scan the pages of the Bible for conclusions on scientific matters. The church has again withdrawn, and left a certain territory free of dogmatic presuppositions and open to the spirit of unfettered enquiry. And with this particular withdrawal, the field of enquiry is immensely widened. No longer is it necessary for each new scientific technique to fight its own battle, to conquer its own territory. Psychology can now investigate the religious consciousness, sociology can study the conditions of racial salvation, and anthropology can set moral codes side by side and analyse them as if they were chemical substances; and all this without any danger of a mass onslaught from the forces of Christendom. The war, as a war, is over for ever, and none but the ignorant on both 'sides' would wish to see it revived.

A word of caution is necessary at this point. It is necessary, if these complex issues are to be handled at all in this short space, to use the imagery of war, 'sides' and 'parties' and the conquest of 'territory'. The parties were not at any time, however, organized groups of committed believers. The scientists were men as well as scientists, and they were often troubled about the apparent implications of their discovery; and the Church, though it gave the impression of being closed to new knowledge, numbered among its members those who were troubled because their beliefs seemed to deny the facts. But though this is true, there is a sense in which the conflict was then like a war and is so no longer. For while it raged it had an external existence. Many Churchmen who were troubled kept silent out of loyalty. Many scientists attacked the Christian position with all the weapons of polemic that they could muster. And though the conflict was then, as always, a conflict in men's hearts, it was for a time projected, as it were, onto a public battlefield. There was a Christian point of view, and there was a scientific point of view; and for a time they became battlecries; though men on both 'sides' felt the force of the truth on the other. This external war is over now partly because we have all of us gained in humility.

The Christian intransigeance arose from the assumption that by reason of a revelation made once and for all, the church knew everything. The scientific intransigeance arose from the assumption that by reason of the limitless powers of the human mind, we should soon know everything. Hard facts have brought home to both parties the truth that we know very little, and that the business of living a life will in all probability continue to be conducted against a background of ignorance and uncertainty.

Even the sum total of human knowledge cannot yet be said to touch more than a small part of what 'living' involves; and as this total expands it becomes more and more difficult for any single human being to grasp at a significant fraction of it; so that if the race knew everything, a single member of it would know nothing.

Allied with this in working towards harmony is the slow growth of a positive welcome to the increase of knowledge. The long struggle caused both parties to suspect the very methods and ends of their opponents, and as the scientists regarded religious thinking as superstition, so the Christian apologists feared scientific thinking as tending to pride and arrogance and self-reliance. Christians knew, from the facts of their own spiritual growth, that such arrogance was a dangerous spiritual state, and they fell unwittingly into the pride of attacking pride.

That mood has changed, now that all, Christian and non-Christian alike, realize with horror just how little we can be proud of knowledge that we do not know how to use: and it is not now knowledge that we fear, but knowledge that is not subdued and controlled by good ends. We should welcome knowledge now without fear, and seek it out, acutely conscious as we are that the knowledge which scientific techniques may offer us is still not all we need. We can split the atom: but no calculation of weight or length or energy will tell us how to apply the perilous force we hold in our hands. And here, in this very thought, lies the distinction between science and religion which is at the heart of the agreement – if such a positive word may be used of the truce that exists today – between the erstwhile warring forces. Science has given up hope of discovering what are called final causes, the ultimate ends of existence which the philosophers seeks to define; and this withdrawal has been to the good of science, which may now proceed about its own business with greater efficiency and assurance. Religion has given up in turn efficient causes, the working of cause and effect in the physical sphere, and has abandoned the habit of *a priori* thinking from dogmatic presuppositions, to the corresponding improvement of religion. And man can now take his place in the Christian conception as a being who is meant to know what he can. In this he gains in dignity, for instead of hiding from knowledge and clinging to superstition he faces frankly the need for searching out what he can find, and acting freely and responsibly according to his knowledge. The world is no longer the magic place of the fairy tales, in which man's choices may be frustrated and flouted by the whims of an uncontrollable and irresponsible deity. He can still be frustrated and flouted, but his enemies are his ignorance of nature and his own weakness and irresponsibility. As he reduces his ignorance he becomes more responsible, more capable of deliberate choices that will work themselves out in action according to his will.

The modern Christian sees no harm in this. God does not claim the service of a fool, or the obedience of one who does not know why he obeys. If man is made for God, his mind as well as his body is God's and he makes the worthier offering if he puts at God's disposal a mind equipped to be used worthily. Devotion is none the less devotion for being intelligent, and love none the less lovely for being enlightened.

There is thus no longer any issue which can be described specifically as lying between 'science' and 'religion'; but there is still a certain tendency to divergence which is active enough to cause misunderstanding, and which I must now briefly examine. The distinction between science and religion, I have said, is between efficient and final causes, between means and ends, between how the universe behaves and why it is there at all. But as science has extended its empire, during the past few hundred years, it has involved all of us in a progressive increase in the amount of time we think scientifically. Matters which were at one time included in the sphere of religion are now taken away and subjected to scientific analysis: the function of the stars, the method of creation, many elements in the development of character, disease, the weather, and countless other aspects of human experience. As we spend more of our time thinking scientifically, we develop a tendency to go on doing so, and to think 'scientifically' (though now the true scientist would disown us) about matters beyond the reach of the scientific method. A close, sustained preoccupation with machines produces a mechanical mind, more interested in how the machine works than in what it is for. The adolescent attitude to motor-bicycles is the type of this kind of thinking, a fascination with the mechanism of the toy and a passion for putting it through its paces rather than a coherent attempt to subordinate a piece of mechanical labour-saving to the larger ends of human purpose. Thus the medieval thinker looked upon the universe as a treasure house full of the evidence of God: the modern thinker is so accustomed to looking at it as a piece of intricate machinery that he cannot see God in it at all; he studies it with instruments that could not reveal God, and then concludes that God is not there; as if he should photograph it in black and white until he concluded that colour did not exist.

It was the temptation of this mechanistic habit of thought that beset George Fox as long ago as 1648, when

> One morning as I was sitting by the fire, a great cloud came over me, and a temptation beset me; but I sate still. And it was said, 'All things come by nature'; and the elements and the stars came over me, so that I was in a manner quite clouded with it.°

It is an experience common enough in the present generation, that 'the elements and the stars' come over us, and it is said, 'All things come by nature.'

This is no longer a theme for controversy, because the scientist, *as such*, no longer claims that what he cannot see cannot be seen. If an expert were to examine a standing car, he could tell us much about how it was constructed, and make a partial guess at some of its purposes; but he could not tell where it was going to next. And in the same way the scientist can tell us a great deal of how the world is constructed, and throw some uncertain light on some of the human purposes which would seem consonant with what he has discovered; but he cannot begin to tell us where the whole process is leading. And if he cannot, as a scientist, prove the truth of religion, he can no more, as a scientist, prove it false. When Napoleon reproached Laplace for not making reference to God in his work on celestial mechanics, the scientist replied, 'Sire, I have no need of that hypothesis.' And Bertrand Russell, arguing that the theory of evolution could not be used by Christian apologists in support of their argument, says, 'From evolution, so far as our present knowledge shows, no ultimately optimistic philosophy can be validly inferred.'°° Both were entirely justified; but neither goes on to claim what *would* be unjustified, that 'that hypothesis' is therefore disproved, or that an 'ultimately optimistic philosophy' is therefore untenable. These beliefs are of a different order, and are held on different grounds, from the hypotheses of the scientist.

°*Journal.*
°°*Religion and Science.*

But though the ultimate objects of the two fields of thought are thus acknowledged to be different, it is not easy to spend a great deal of time in the study of the one without beginning to undervalue the other. The tune that one has just learnt tends to sing itself on in the mind, and the search for one kind of knowledge and belief tends to exclude the search for another. So modern man, skilled in the use of one set of intellectual tools, allows another to rust.

But in truth, they are both necessary. We cannot live without our science now: there is no turning back on knowledge. It has provided us with the means of our present life, and without it we could not live. But though it is an indispensable means, it still offers no guidance on the ends of that life. It only furnishes us means utilizable for ends. It does not indicate the ends themselves. And this is true even of its own end, the very motive of scientific study. It is said that the scientific motive is pure curiosity; but pure curiosity would not carry us far unless it were sustained by a belief in purpose. Ultimately we can only search for meaning; and we could not for long look for meaning if we were convinced that the whole thing was meaningless. And the scientists themselves are always among the first to step out of their narrow rôle when their discoveries raise large issues outside themselves, to stand up as human beings and make the issues clear. It was the scientists who had made the atom bomb who were the first to demand that this new force should be subdued and subordinated to intelligent purpose: before the churches, before the statesmen, before the philosophers. And in doing that they spoke not as scientists but as men with a concern for ends beyond science.

The same is true with another habit of thought that the scientific method imposes on us: the habit of demanding a particular kind of proof. There is now an established manner of seeking evidence and presenting it and judging it which by convention has acquired the prestige of 'proof'. Any other kind of evidence remains a matter of probability, of opinion. We rightly develop the habit, then, of asking, 'What is the evidence? And is it valid? Is it demonstrable in terms which men everywhere will accept?' This is right and proper when we deal with things that are indeed demonstrable in those terms. But human life is larger than the laboratory, and we are compelled to live by probabilities in the ordinary life of human relations, and in the choices we make day by day. We cannot demonstrate that a friendship will be profitable and creative except by embracing it: we cannot 'prove' it. We cannot demonstrate that we are marrying the right girl, except by going on without proof. And even at the end of life we should be hard put to it to demonstrate to anyone else – and that is of the essence of scientific proof – that the friendship had been a successful one, or that we had indeed married the right girl.

We cannot live, indeed, without the ultimately 'optimistic philosophy' which cannot be inferred from the theory of evolution. The doctor knows all his patients are condemned to death, but must work on the assumption that they are not. Parents have children knowing that some children born to them or their neighbours must die on the roads, or if they survive grow up delinquent, or mad, or incurably diseased; yet they must act in the hope that their children will be safe from these things. And as this is true of these limited choices, it is also true of the ultimate attitude to life which each of us, however incoherently we may have framed it, must perforce maintain as we live. There are indications to the contrary, yet we must hope; and the very hope is the only answer to these indications to the contrary. If what we cannot prove is untrue, then we cannot live. We need the 'ends' if we are to use the means.

A special aspect of this problem of proof lies in the scientist's use of experiment. He demonstrates his hypothesis by claiming that if certain conditions are observed, certain things will happen; not once, but twice and thrice, and as often as the conditions are repeated. And he tests his own thinking at every point by a demonstration of this sort. Here again habit takes hold. One cannot spend one's working hours saying, 'Let's try it and see', without developing a tendency to take the same attitude to fields of experience in which the method will no longer hold. It has thus become fashionable to regard an 'experimental ethic' as inevitably healthier and more progressive than a 'dogmatic ethic' (and indeed, these two words, experimental and dogmatic have become invested with heavy overtones of emotional meaning, the one signifying 'alert, open-minded, honest, forward-looking'; the other 'authoritarian, dictatorial, prejudiced, dishonest and reactionary'). But in truth to experiment with human affairs of any importance is to ignore the fundamental condition of the scientific method. For the scientist demands that the conditions shall be the

same each time the experiment is performed; but when, for example, sexual experiment takes place, the conditions can never be
the same again. The participants are both different for it, and can
never go back. The same is true of almost any 'experiment' in
human affairs, except for the most trivial. We cannot study the
effect of capital punishment by experimental methods, because
we can never know how the criminal would have behaved if he
had not been beheaded. We cannot even experiment seriously in
education, because no two 'control' groups are ever quite the
same.

And overriding these technical objections is the supreme refusal
to have humanity treated as so much neutral matter. We will not
execute this criminal and not that, nor bring up one child this
way and another that, just for the sake of increasing our knowledge. We will not even make use of the knowledge that men do
sometimes procure in this way, and we suppress the documents
of Buchenwald. Personality is in some sense indestructible, and
we cannot let it be regarded as anything less. These are limits on
the scientific method which we all recognize, and obey without
hesitation. In less serious matters it is common enough to think
of experiment as a proper method of the study of humanity:
and so it is, but only subject to the recognition of human values
that lie beyond its scope.

There are thus these three ways in which the scientific habit of
thought is inapplicable to the higher purposes of human life.
First, its mechanistic presuppositions, which cannot be applied to
the use to which the machine is put; second, the nature of proof,
wholly inapplicable to the probabilities by which we are compelled to live; and the habit of experiment, which can never
reach far enough to encompass the ends of life. Religious thought
may thus proceed to deal with a field of experience which
scientific thought cannot touch. Does this mean that religion is
wholly unscientific, and that the scientist must put away all he
has learnt when he turns to these ultimate problems?

This would be a tempting conclusion if we were desirous of
avoiding the tension and conflict of thought which has in the
past always arisen on the borders between science and religion.
It would be pleasant to dismiss the whole problem as irrelevant,
and to say that some matters demand a wholly scientific treatment
and others a wholly religious one. But the solution is not really so
simple. Religion and science are not dealing with different fields

of experience, but with the same fields from different points of view and by different methods. Their conclusions may not overlap to any large extent, but it is intolerable that they should conflict; and as long as there is any apparent conflict, the tension of mind must continue. We cannot divorce means from ends, nor the part from the whole. And to say that science deals with means, or the part, and religion with ends, or the whole, is but to emphasize how inextricably mixed up they are together – as the medieval churchmen, indeed, rightly realized.

It is urgent to bear this conclusion in mind when we look back and acknowledge how much religious thinking has in the end owed to the science that at first appeared its enemy. The victory of the Copernican system was a victory for true religion as well as true science; not only because true thinking is always better religion than ignorance, but because it permitted Christian thought to purge itself of elements that made it less Christian than it ought to be. True Christianity has never been under the illusion that man was the centre of the universe; and though the medieval system did not claim that this was true in the moral sense (and may indeed be said to argue the opposite, since earth, though at the centre of the universe, was at the most distant point from God, who was all round it) yet the whole mechanism of planets and influences put man in a place that ministered unhealthily to his self-regard. The establishment of the principle of mechanism, the idea that the machine was in fact a machine and behaved like one, permitted many moral and spiritual advances that would have been difficult without it: the withering of the belief in witchcraft, so that no longer could eccentric old women be burnt because it was thought they had raised a storm or murdered a neighbour with a waxen image and a needle; or the growing acceptance of lunacy as a disease to be treated with love instead of a possession to be exorcised with cruelty; these and other gains have sprung from what at the time was regarded as a secularization of thought.

Christian thought has gained too from the increasing habit of looking for scientific proof, for regarding as a tentative hypothesis certain matters which it is now obvious we shall never be in a position to demonstrate by any method that will carry overwhelming conviction. We are thus better off without impassioned sermons threatening us with hell fire in eternal punishment for our sins and the contradiction of the use of fear to evoke love.

There are still those who fear hell, but not now many to threaten others with it; and part of this new gentleness we owe to the opening of our eyes to the fact that we know nothing whatever about it, nor are likely to this side of the grave.

Christianity owes less, perhaps, to the experimental method than it does to the general habits of thought, because, as I have argued, human affairs are less susceptible to experimental demonstration than physical structure. But as experimental psychology develops its techniques, they will be used more and more in the service of the whole rehabilitation of man which is the fruit of the religious endeavour.

Religion has thus not only nothing to fear from the growth of science, but has already owed much to science for the furthering of her own purposes, the deepening of her own understanding. But after all is that not what we should expect? If we stop thinking in terms of 'religion' and 'science', using the words as if they were the names of political parties, and instead think of 'man knowing' and 'man worshipping'; is it not to be expected that knowledge will help him in his worship? Primitive religion is inferior to a highly developed one, not because primitive men are morally perverted, but because they are ignorant. It is sometimes the habit among Christians to be suspicious of learning, but it is not learning that is the danger but the pride of learning, the notion that learning is all one needs, and the equation of spiritual with intellectual discernment. The fact of the matter is that the one *serves* the other, the mind supports the spirit. Means are worthless without ends, and that is why science alone is not enough; but ends cannot be reached without means, and that is why religion calls for knowledge, full and unprejudiced, of what can be known. You cannot drive a car without going somewhere; but equally you cannot drive without the car.

The issue today is no longer between two agencies, fighting each other for the possession of a particular piece of ground. It is a personal issue for every man, to subordinate his habits of thought to the total ends of human life, to ensure that his knowledge leads to understanding and his thinking to wisdom; and likewise to endeavour that his understanding and wisdom, his judgement on the ends of life, take into account the facts which can be known.

CHAPTER THREE

The Effect of Psychology

THE open war between 'science' and 'religion' is now widely agreed to be over, but when an individual comes to grips with the problems which are, properly speaking, the sphere of religion, he still finds the prestige of science so great that he finds it difficult to pass beyond it. And though the physical sciences no longer raise serious difficulties in his mind, the new science of psychology, taking as its field of operation the activity of mind itself, raises obstacles to religious thinking which many men have found insuperable. The power of the new challenge lies in this, that if religious ideas can be demonstrated to have a physical cause, they can no longer have a spiritual significance; and if the experiences of the mind can be shown to be determined by causes as mechanical as the sensations of the body, then the activities of the mind, including its religious ideals, are as mechanical and insignificant as the lower functions of the body. Or to put it more simply, if scientists can 'explain' religion, then they can explain it away.

Here is indeed a challenge more fundamental than any that has in the past been offered by physicist or biologist. In the scientific and tolerant temper of the age, it has not exploded into open war. But that is because both 'sides' know their own business better than they did in the past, and there are too many informed men who are already on both 'sides' at the same time, who appreciate religious values that reach beyond their clinical experience; and the numerous clergy who make use of psychological techniques in the practice of their cure of souls. The situation is not favourable to another, futile party struggle on the issue. But that is not to solve the individual tension that arises when a man who is seeking to formulate his religious conceptions finds the way to progress barred by psychologically based doubt. Before I turn to the positive content of Christian experience today, I must therefore turn to the psychological attack on it.

To some extent, the psychologist's challenge is the same as that of any science, and results from the same perpetuation of scientific thinking into the non-scientific sphere. There is, for example, the same tendency to mechanism, now with the name 'behaviourism'. This is based on the new discoveries of the limits on human freedom, hitherto guessed at but not attested, feared but never proved. Psycho-analysis has revealed and many experiments have confirmed, that a large part of our mind, and that an active controlling part of the mind, lies below the surface of consciousness. The subconscious mind is now envisaged not merely as a storehouse of memory, but as a dynamic structure of instinctive drives and impulses which, despite the utmost effort of our conscious will, insist on affecting our thought and action to an enormous extent. We forget something, for example, that we consciously 'want' to remember; but it is often because subconsciously we 'want' to forget. We 'choose' to do something, but do not realize that our choice is made in the subconscious mind, and often for very different reasons from those we should admit. Or we are ill because, unknown to our conscious self, we 'want' to be ill. These concepts have passed into our common assumptions now, and are part of the intellectual air we breathe, and work upon our conclusions about the very value of the choices we make. Much more, too, is known about the limitations imposed upon us by our heredity, which we recognize as laying down certain limits on both the extent and nature of our later achievement. We cannot greatly increase our intelligence, nor change an aptitude. Our range of choice is laid down narrowly at birth. And after birth the early days of infancy define yet more sharply the road along which we shall travel. One child, stunted and starved of affection, is fated to be a criminal in later life; another, overwhelmed by indulgent affection, is destined to make extravagant claims on life, and to develop a neurosis. Or one intelligence is provided with the knowledge and skill that are the tools of its exercise; and another is left undeveloped, to atrophy and die. Is the ignorant fool 'free' to behave intelligently? Is the child whose infancy was twisted 'free' to straighten his life out again in adolescence? And if these lives may be shown to be inevitable, are we not all in some measure limited by similar influences? And can a religious belief that involves some measure of freedom to the human soul be tenable?

There are two clear answers to this particular aspect of the modern doubt. The first is that it is not as modern as it looks.

It is now cast in a psychological form, but it is no more than the old argument between determinism and free will, which in some form or other has been with man as long as he has thought at all. If God knows everything, it ran at one time, he knows what will happen tomorrow. If he knows what will happen tomorrow, that happening is already determined, and I am not free to choose. It was this aspect of the problem that Milton's devils debated while they awaited the issue of Satan's assault upon earth, reasoning

> Of Providence, Foreknowledge, Will, and Fate,
> Fixt Fate, free will, foreknowledge absolute,
> And found no end, in wandring mazes lost.°

This is an old doubt in a new form; and like many old doubts, it is not to be easily dismissed or glibly answered. We *are* greatly limited in the freedom of our choice by the events of the past; but we cannot escape the conviction that human life takes its significance, not from the limitations to its freedom, but from the element of freedom within its limitations. We must behave as if, in the end, we had responsibility, or all is lost.

The second answer is that as in the physical sciences the extension of knowledge is itself making a mechanistic account less acceptable; and there are no more trenchant attacks on behaviourism to be found than those by non-behaviourist psychologists. There are elements in human experience which prove the less yielding to the laws of simple cause and effect the more we understand them; and there are choices that men are able to make which seem wholly inexplicable in terms of the behaviourist theory.

The truth is that religious experience must have some sort of physical manifestation. Man is a being with physical existence, and his understanding of his own end and destiny must affect that physical existence, must be felt, as it were, on the pulse. But the fact that any experience has a physical element does not mean that it has no more. A picture is more than the sum total of paint, canvas, vibrations, and muscular movements that go to make it; and religious experience is greater than the physical changes that might accompany it. What the artist sees in a landscape is not rendered valueless because we can explain scientifically how the landscape came to be there; and religious insight is not to be

°*Paradise Lost* Book II, p.559-61.

dismissed by the explanation of how it was achieved. The view from the top of a mountain is not to be 'explained away' by an account of how we had to climb to get it.

The mechanism of religious experience is quite properly a field of scientific enquiry, and as we learn more about it, we may hope that our religion will be the purer and truer, as it has become purer and truer because of our advancing understanding of physics. But as physics can hold out no hope of throwing light on the final values of life, so the study of psychological mechanism can hope only to show *how* the mind works, and can as yet offer no hope of illuminating why and to what end it should work. Even the mind is but a means to an ulterior end which gives it significance; and here as always, science is concerned with the means and not the end.

The same considerations apply to the experimental approach which psychology, like all sciences, has to adopt. It is too early to say much of the possible scope of experimental psychology. Hitherto it has been confined – or at least its results have been confined – to matters of comparatively little importance. It would be presumptuous to say this must always be so; yet it is difficult to see how it is to attack important issues without losing its experimental character. We can observe what happens to a mind when the brain is attacked by disease or a wound; but we cannot cut the brain away just to see what happens. We can study the effects on a growing child of a fall on the head; but we cannot drop children on their heads, as Galileo dropped his lumps of metal, just to find out what we want to know. We are held in the grip of our value-judgements here, and cannot lay them on one side to experiment until we find some more. This has been manifested recently in the anxiety that has arisen over the performance of the operation of leucotomy, which the surgeons have developed from the highest of motives, but which involves such deep alteration of the personality that there is widespread demand that it should be subordinated to the closest scrutiny.

It is, as I have said, too early to tell how far this new technique of experimental psychology will take us; but it is not too early to affirm that it must be contained within a large view of human destiny. We may observe man by any technique we please; we may experiment on him in ways that do not reach very deep; but as soon as we begin to touch the central issues of personality in a way which is irrevocable or irretraceable, we have to return to a mode of thought which is more properly religious than scientific. This is no issue between friends of religion and friends of psychology: it lies between the friends and foes of humanity, between those who accept – as doctors have done throughout the centuries – the inescapable and impregnable value of human life, and those who would treat some men as 'expendable' in the interests of the learning and comfort of the rest.

The fundamental scientific presuppositions of psychology are thus to be accepted as of the same order of value as the corresponding presuppositions of physics or biology. But there is a particular aspect of the psychological attack on religion which needs special consideration: that which originated in the work of the psycho-analysts. The name to conjure with here is that of Freud, who is popularly suspected of having exploded religion by tracing it all back to the unfulfilled dreams of infancy. This simple statement of the result of his work would satisfy neither Freud himself nor the many Christian psychologists who have found the large element of truth in Freud's observations of enormous value to them in the work of their pastorate.* But apart from the dangerous effect of half-knowledge in such matters, and the widespread acceptance of Freudian doctrine by those who have never read a line of his writings, there is undeniably a serious challenge here to religious thought.

The argument runs that religious experience is but a shadow of man's desires, caused by two tendencies of the mind known as projection and regression. Projection is the habit of seeing what we want to see, and shaping reality according to our needs. Regression is the tendency to return, when our needs are not met, to the images of childhood, making dreams in our helplessness of the things which in the time of our greatest helplessness used to satisfy our needs. Freud thus claimed that psycho-analysis had traced the origin of religion to the helplessness of childhood, and its content to the persistence of the wishes and needs of childhood. Hence the father-image, the figure of the all-powerful who yet need not be feared, because he is all loving. And in tune with the centrality for Freud's thought of the sexual function, he pressed on to suggest that religion was an 'aberration of the sexual function', because of its use of erotic symbolism, its frequent appearance in adolescence, and the like.

But none of this proves anything at all. The use of the 'pro-

*See R. S. Lee: *Freud and Christianity.*

jection' theory simply admits that man needs God: it neither proves nor disproves the existence of God. When a man is hungry, he may dream of food; and his dream is an illusion. But the fact that it arises from his need of food does not prove that the whole concept of food is based on illusion: it says nothing either way about the existence of food. And the same argument applies to the charge that religion is regression to father-fixation. The fact that man's need of good, loving purpose is clothed in the imagery of fatherhood does not prove that there is no good, loving purpose to meet his needs. He chooses one plain need with its plain answer as the symbol of his belief that another need, less plain but more far-reaching, has its answer too. The one is the symbol of the other: but the explanation of the choice of a symbol does not prove the falsity of the thing symbolized.

The specific attribution of religious aspiration to frustrated sexuality is the subject of a footnote to William James's *The Varieties of Religious Experience.*

> It seems to me that few conceptions are less instructive than this re-interpretation of religion as perverted sexuality. It reminds one, so crudely is it often employed, of the famous Catholic taunt, that the Reformation may be best understood by remembering that its *fons et origo* was Luther's wish to marry a nun: —the effects are infinitely wider than the alleged causes, and for the most part opposite in nature. It is true that in the vast collection of religious phenomena, some are undisguisedly amatory—e.g., sex-deities, and obscene rites in polytheism, and ecstatic feelings of union with the Saviour in a few Christian mystics. But then why not equally call religion an aberration of the digestive function, and prove one's point by the worship of Bacchus and Ceres, or by the ecstatic feelings of some other saints about the Eucharist? Religious language clothes itself in such poor symbols as our life affords, and the whole organism gives overtones of comment whenever the mind is strongly stirred to expression. Language drawn from eating and drinking is probably as common in religious literature as is language drawn from the sexual life. We 'hunger and thirst' after righteousness; we 'find the Lord a sweet savour'; we 'taste and see that he is good'. 'Spiritual milk for American babes, drawn from the breasts of both testaments,' is a sub-title of the once famous New England Primer, and Christian devotional literature quite floats in milk, thought of from the point of view, not of the mother, but of the greedy babe.

And to the argument that the religious life awakens in adolescence, and for that reason must be an aspect of the sexual awakening he replies,

> To which the retort again is easy. Even were the asserted synchrony unrestrictedly true as a fact (which it is not), it is not only the sexual life,

but the entire higher mental life which awakens during adolescence. One might then as well set up the thesis that the interest in mechanics, physics, chemistry, logic, philosophy, and sociology, which springs up during adolescent years along with that in poetry and religion, is also a perversion of the sexual instinct: —but that would be too absurd.

These specific arguments can, indeed, all be met, point by point as they are pressed. But in terms of the current thought of our time, they are but aspects of a dark widespread suspicion that our consciousness is no longer to be trusted: our very thought is a dishonest way of justifying our desires.

There are two answers to this. In the first place, it is an argument, like all scientific, 'logical' argument, that leaves the issue unresolved. If our religious beliefs are mere rationalization of desire for security, atheistic beliefs may be mere rationalization of desire for freedom. One man may yearn for the lost security of his childhood, and thus invent a religious system that seems to provide it; another man may be haunted by fear of his father and may invent a religious system which has no God, no ultimate responsibility, no ultimate standards, to comfort himself against the fear of responsibility with which he had grown up. The argument thus cuts both ways, and can be made to seem equally plausible as a destructive agency on either side. A young man once advanced this argument to the late Archbishop Temple, in these words: 'You only believe what you do believe because of your early upbringing.' And Dr. Temple replied, 'But you only believe that I believe what I believe because of my early upbringing because of your early upbringing.' It is but one more argument that fails to prove anything.

But there is a further consideration which renders rationalization an incomplete account of any religious aspiration, and particularly the Christian formulation of it. For can any honest man describe the religious struggle as 'wish-fulfilment'? Angels, and 'pie in the sky', perhaps yes; but no religion, and least of all the Christian, has ever made much of that. The essence of all religious life is an effort to control the lower impulses in the interests of the higher, to hold in their place the very desires which are said to be rationalized. The Cross and the martyr's fire are not 'rationalizations' of bodily desire. And if one side or the other may be considered the more likely to be indulging in rationalization, it is surely the side which argues that nothing matters; that we may live as we please, eat, drink and be merry, for tomorrow we die and are swept into oblivion; and nothing we did for good or ill counts any more, except in terms of a little happiness or misery for those who survive us. This is surely the 'tempting' belief, the system that would release our desires and give them free play, or at least freedom limited only by a few obvious rules of common sense. It is easy to see how a man could rationalize this longing for indulgence, and turn his microscope upon the world, and say he sees no god; and measure and weigh, and say he finds no god; and scan the vast spaces of the sky, and say he finds no god.

Rationalization is a two-edged weapon, which cannot cut one side without wounding the other. But is that not the truth, in the end, about the entire effort to apply scientific criteria to the field of religious enquiry? I have argued that organized religion has gained immensely from the progress of science; and that is true; but it has not gained because science has been able to throw light on the proper business of religion. It has gained only because science has robbed religion of what was never its proper business. The same process will continue, now with less bitterness, it is to be hoped, but with equal firmness on the part of the scientists, and similar benefit to the church, as they pursue their ruthless way. Psychology has many thefts to make yet: clearing up the border-line between knowledge and ignorance, certainty and faith, whether it be in the value of prayer, or the use of faith-healing, or the clearing of the ground for a new moral judgement on mental disease, or the relations of the sexes, or the sexual drive itself. There is nothing to be feared from the invasion of science here, any more than there was anything to fear from the conquests of physics or biology. For science means nothing more nor less than a certain kind of knowledge; a limited certainty; a technique of finding out a part of the living environment with which we have to deal. But when we know all we can know, it is still a condition of our life that we must act by beliefs about what we do not know.

None of the great arguments of the past, by which the existence of God was demonstrated, can be regarded as conclusive, in the sense that they oppress the mind of all men equally with a conviction that they cannot escape; but none of the great arguments *against* the existence of God is any more convincing. And modern science is like all the rest. It has thrown light on many dark corners, and has revealed to be dark other corners that men in their arrogance claimed were light. But it has gone no further; and on the ultimate question of what is light and what is dark, it has no word to say.

Does this mean, then, that religion is a mere whim? And that these questions of ultimate significance and value are matters of taste alone, irrelevant to our life because, even if they *are* representative of what is true, they are unknowable and inapplicable? Is God so completely the Eternal Other that man can know nothing of him? Is light so far away that man is utterly in the dark? If he is, then the sensible thing to do is to return again to the 'eat and drink' argument. God exists, but has nothing to do with us; or, God exists, but has left us so completely without knowledge of him that we must get along as well as we can under the guidance of idle desires of the moment.

We do not make this choice in other spheres of experience where scientific knowledge is similarly irrelevant. We cannot prove that we are marrying the right girl; but we do not for that reason marry no girl at all. We cannot prove that this picture is better than that, but we buy it for our house all the same. We cannot demonstrate the value of friendship, but we continue to cultivate it. And in all these matters we are guided by a mixture of values that include many that cannot be described or demonstrated in terms that other men will accept without dispute; and which yet – and here is the point – will be widely accepted. There are certain values in human life which men recognize as applicable over a wide field, and as probably representing some wide truth which stands on firmer ground than whim or desire. We differ about what is beautiful, but we agree that despite our differences there is, present somewhere, beauty that is safe from our argument. We make our judgements on each other, and choose our friends; and we may be proved wrong in the judgement we made, but not in our belief that the judgement *had* to be made, and that had we been better informed and better judges, we might have made better judgements.

However we may batter our mind against the uncertainties on the fringe of our knowledge, we know that we must act as if certain things were true about the very uncertainty itself: and we make our choices responsibly, carefully, believing that the more we know, the better judges we are, the more likely we are to be right. It is not all pure chance, with our reliability never to be increased beyond that of the spun coin. There are, we are convinced, realities beyond the microscope and the callipers which we can begin dimly to see. But we see them with our own eyes, and come at them by a judgement of our whole personality, all our knowledge and hope and way of thought and way of living: they are all involved in this kind of perception.

Now there is a great difference in reliability between this kind of judgement of the whole personality and mere whim. We may say, 'I like that,' or 'I don't believe that,' and be hopelessly wrong, because only a mood or a fragment of the mind is at work. But when we have searched and pondered, and our minds are stored with all the knowledge we can muster and practised in making judgements and habituated to the perception of values; then we can still be wrong, but we have more likelihood of being right. The chance visitor who drops into the National Gallery and pronounces in ignorance and arrogance on the virtues of the pictures will probably be no more 'right' than he would have been if he threw a dice. But the critic who has studied and thought and argued and listened, though he may still be perverse, will have more chance of making the judgements which other men will recognize as valid. We cannot go further than this: but nor does the scientist. When he produces his evidence, it is cast in such a form that other men will recognize it as valid. Place the ruler alongside, he will say, and it will always show a length of ten inches. But if a generation were to arise which obstinately refused to recognize ten inches for what it was, then science would be no more valid than palmistry.

These personal judgements, then, on which religious belief must always in the end rely, are not entirely private, or unrelated to other men's standards of belief. When one man describes a landscape, another man can hear him and catch something of the meaning of what he is saying: and can verify it by looking for himself. And the same is true of religion: when some men talk of their vision of the things that matter, we recognize stirrings of our own personality in response, we feel we understand something of what they are talking about. And we, too, can look for ourselves, and see something of what they have seen. We find ourselves talking in some measure the same language.

There are certain tests we should apply to this kind of talk together about experience that goes beyond the merely demonstrable, tests which must be applied to religious belief as to all accounts of personal experience. We must ask, first, that the experience should not conflict with what we know in other ways: that religion should not contradict the plain facts of science, for example. Our belief about what is beyond knowledge must not deny the knowledge we possess, it must cohere.

It must be congruent not only with the 'known facts', but with the experience of others. If all men say a field is green, the experience that leads to the conclusion it is blue must be regarded as suspect. We are thus entitled to demand that religious belief should take into account whatever is known about the world, and what different men have believed about it, the facts and half-facts, certainties and hopes, which form the groundwork of hypothesis. And this is one of the services which science has rendered, in insisting that the facts, at all events, be taken seriously.

We are also entitled to ask that the religious belief should have a certain relevance, some measure of usefulness, if you like, in offering a helpful explanation of the universe. The medieval poser, How many angels can stand on the point of a pin? is not such a belief, and can be regarded as strictly irrelevant. Men, even young men, would be better employed turning their dialectical skill in other directions, as we should all now agree. But there are still to be heard arguments on matters which would not affect either our general understanding or our final conclusion, debates on the *trivia* of religious speculation which engender heat, but leave the issue dark.

We may further press the question, of any account of personal experience, What sort of a person has had this experience? If one man says a field is grey, we ask if he is colour blind; and when a man tells his story of the meaning of life, we must ask if he lives it healthily. Does he see what other men see in less debatable fields? Is he free from prejudice or mental disease? Is he one who is given to rationalization? This, any more than any other test, is not complete in itself. Good health is not a guarantee of a knowledge of the truth, nor the efficient conduct of business a warrant of a grasp of ultimate reality. Nor, on the other hand, is ineffectiveness in one sphere a certain indication of falsehood in another. An artist may be great though his personal relationships with his own family are petty; and religious genius, no less than other forms of genius, may be consonant with a marked lack of balance or many-sidedness. But in practice we are all enormously influenced by this consideration: there is, we come to recognize, a quality of wisdom, ripeness, fullness, integrity, which carries

weight in the discussion of the intangibles of human life. There
are men who live what they believe with such openness and
fullness that their beliefs come home to us. What they do is so
golden that we must take seriously the reason of their doing it.

And as this is true of men we have known in our own lives, it
it true of men who have left the story of their deeds and their
beliefs on the page of history. And because of this, we treat the
beliefs of Napoleon as interesting but irrelevant; while the beliefs
of Tolstoi we are driven to take seriously – critically, open to
correction, but still seriously. And within the Christian experience,
this test of personality drives us back at once, and continually, to
the whole personality of Jesus. If this man is as haunting and
persuasive as he has been found to be, then his beliefs may need
to be taken seriously; if he seems to be a true man, then his
beliefs may be true beliefs. The essential question here is, What
think ye of Christ? Was he in some way what he said he was?
Did he import into human life something of the truth about the
eternal things? Or was he just wrong? Was his life based on an
illusion or a deception? Was he mad, or a fraud?

These are questions just as urgent as the questions the scientist
asks in his laboratory, and may be approached with the same
honesty of purpose and hope of the 'right', as distinct from a
merely individual, whimsical answer, as the scientist's. And to ask
them is to ask, in the strictest sense, a scientific question. It is the
first question a psychologist would ask if a man were brought to
him with a strange story: Is he mad, or is he a fraud? No increase
in our knowledge of madness will ever release the psychologist
from having to make up his mind on all the evidence: however
much he knows, there will always remain the possibility that the
man who says he has seen a miracle has really seen it. And as the
psychologist must ask this question in his consulting room if he
is to be a 'whole' scientist, so we must ask it if we are to be
whole men. There is nothing clever in ignoring some of the facts;
and to ignore the challenge of Jesus and the history of Christian
experience is to ignore facts. They may, in the end, be rejected;
and honest men have, after due deliberation, so rejected them.
But they cannot be merely left alone. To ignore what the best
men have said, but cannot prove, is as intellectually contemptible
as to cling to beliefs that clever men have exploded (provided
they really *have* exploded them, and not merely made a loud
noise and covered them in dust). And if the modern trend towards

the study of personality as a whole entity leads anywhere, it must surely lead to this, that the beliefs of those men and women in history who impress us as having the most rounded and firmly based personalities must be taken seriously, even when they cannot be revealed by our little instruments.

In the end our beliefs about the ultimate value of man are bound up with our beliefs about his daily living; and our *beliefs* about daily living are not theory or techniques of thought but systems of personal behaviour – mental, physical, emotional behaviour. They are all tied together, these things, in a response to reality made by a whole person. That is why scientific techniques are not enough, though they are part; why reason is not enough, though it is a part. If a man hopes to reach down to a large understanding, he must use the whole of himself, the power of observation, measurement, and description; and also the power of taking a stand on ground he has not yet been able fully to survey. He must, as it were, live by his beliefs before he has had time to test them, before he has even found a way of testing them. For it is the living that presses on him as urgent; and it is the living, moreover, that tests the belief. A religion – and equally an irreligion – is a choice of beliefs about the meaning of human personality, a decision on whether it means anything or nothing. And we are making that choice in action every day, even when we refuse to face it in theory.

To the rationalist who argues that religion is out of date because it is based on dogma while science is based on first hand observation we are then entitled to claim that he amass all the facts of his observation, scientific and supra-scientific, the facts of observation and the facts of value; and 'dogma' is one of the facts of value. It is a judgement on experience, an interpretation of what men have dimly glimpsed beyond the things that can be shown to be. The day has passed when dogma was a clear system of conviction which men had to accept on authority, whatever they had found out for themselves. And there is within the authentic Christian experience a growing emphasis on the necessity for first-hand experience in this, as in other realms. One such emphasis is provided by the growth of Quakerism, which arose at the height of the scientific movement, and applied to the religious quest the same obstinate desire for personal conviction and integrity as the scientist applied to his study of the world. Some aspects of the relationship between the two will be considered at a later stage; but the point of departure is the one I have sought to establish through all this discussion of science and religion, that science is concerned with the part, religion with the whole, science with means, religion with ends; and *therefore* the criteria of validity for religious experience, though open to scrutiny from the techniques of reason, are in the end *personal* criteria. This does not mean they are individual, in the sense that each individual may make his own; it means that each person must respond with the whole of his powers. It is for that reason that the central fact of Quaker experience is the same as that of all Christian experience: the person of Christ himself.

This must be so, for it is only in terms of personality that religion can be expressed with anything approaching completeness. A religious belief is a belief about the significance of the world to human beings; and that relationship, the-world-and-human-beings, can be contained only in an understanding that embraces whole personality. The language of human life is human life itself, as the language of music is music itself. Other language, the symbols of science or speech are but partial, limited, concerned with one aspect of reality at a time. But a language concerned with the whole-at-once must be the language of human living.

This, then, is the point of departure for the next stage of our thought. I have in this brief survey of the scientific mode of thought endeavoured to demonstrate that nothing is proved, nothing can be proved, and that it is a condition of our life as we understand it that nothing should be proved. We can acquire our knowledge and still not know what to do with it. But that is no reason for doing nothing with it. What, then, can we do? Which direction seems to promise the surest road? For different ways vary greatly in the power of their appeal. And all that our techniques of knowledge can do still leave the way open for men to listen to the appeal of Christ.

CHAPTER FOUR

Jesus in the Experience of Men

IT is impossible now, after two thousand years, to recapture fully the impression that Jesus made on his contemporaries. Even his contemporaries, writing in the gospels, cannot do that for us; for they wrote when their lives had been changed by him, and when a community of dedicated people had begun to suffer and die for him. And since they wrote others have written, and people have taken up their positions in relation to certain beliefs about him, interpretations of the universe determined by interpretations of the work and person of Christ. All this makes it impossible to imagine what it was like to be a fisherman or a village woman or a Jewish patriot or a time-server exploiting the wealth and protection of the Roman empire; and to meet by chance in a crowd the man Jesus of Nazareth. Today his name means *something* to us: a childhood memory, pleasant or unpleasant according to the childhood; a bearded, alien figure, irrelevant, unchallenging; an oath; a man who preached wisdom which it would be well if men could follow; a mysterious symbol of mysterious religious ideas – it may be one of these meanings that he carries, but he never comes to us unknown, to arouse our curiosity and set us questioning. Only too often he stands in our minds for a body of people we have met and disliked: a particular congregation which has repelled us, or a whole system of thought and worship which has nauseated us. Or he may stand for an ideal which we already know to be impossible: impossible for us, and plainly impossible for those who preached him to us.

We can never escape too from the knowledge of what men have thought about him: the divinity they have seen in him; the supernatural system they have perceived around him. There would be many to say we should not try. The knowledge of God, they would argue, is conveyed not only by the life and teaching of Jesus, but by the work of Jesus in the lives of men who followed him. What they saw in him is part of his work. He

47

meant, as it were, to work on us by means of the beliefs of men who have gone before us. The Church is thus a living interpreter and complement of the work of Christ: it is the living body of Christ. There is thus no reason to endeavour to recapture the experience of the early followers of Christ, who served him because they saw him, instead of, as we have to do, coming slowly to see him because we serve him.

There are others, however, who would give much to be able to come to the story of Christ fresh and unprejudiced, in the belief that as we stand side by side with those who saw him we should see more of him, because we see him clear, undecorated by the trappings of royalty and undisfigured by the haze of controversy. The division of opinion here is now hardened into a sectarian difference, so that one branch of the church would be known to make one choice and another a different one. Yet it is probably in origin a temperamental distinction: the divergence between those who are taught and then take hold, and those who like to find out for themselves. Dogma and experience are not enemies to each other: the one lays out beliefs for men to see; the other sets men looking for beliefs that will interpret what they have seen. It is only arrogance that makes enemies of them: the arrogance of dogma, that says, This has been revealed to others: you must believe it; or the arrogance of experience, that says, That has not been revealed to me: therefore it is not true.

But though there is no necessary opposition between dogma and experience, there is a necessary choice to be made as to which we would wish to start from. The early Friends claimed that Quakerism was 'primitive Christianity revived'; and that would be the keynote of their study of Jesus, the effort to stand with the early Christians, and pass through the stages of their developing understanding. And though it is now impossible to make ourselves as ignorant of Jesus as the early disciples were before they met him, it is possible to order our thinking about him something after the manner of the disciples' growing understanding; to ask what manner of man this was, instead of asking first what divine purpose he came to fulfil.

Let us then take the story of his life and see what impact he makes on us: what impact he *would* have made on us if we had been there to know him. Let us take a single version of the story, choosing St. Luke's for no better reason than that it is the most attractive narrative; and leaving aside the many points of controversy, historical, exegetical, doctrinal, let us try to put ourselves in the position of the men who saw him first.

The story must begin in the middle of chapter 4,* after the narrative of the birth, which it is clear that men had then not heard; and after the story of the temptations, which must have been disclosed later to one of the disciples. The public life of Jesus thus begins with a sermon in his home village, preached on the text from Isaiah,

> The Spirit of the Lord is upon me, because he hath anointed me to preach the gospel to the poor; he hath sent me to heal the brokenhearted, to preach deliverance to the captives, and recovering of sight to the blind, to set at liberty them that are bruised, to preach the acceptable year of the Lord.

And then, we are told, he sat down (as the preacher in the synagogue did), and said,

> This day is this scripture fulfilled in your ears.

His audience were disturbed by the assurance with which he made this bold claim, and said, 'Is not this Joseph's son?' This was the sort of message which needed a certificate of authority, or at best the prestige of a foreign, unknown face. But for Jesus, a lad of the village, to talk like this – it was intolerable. So they threw him out; and he went on to a village where he was not known, and there, 'they were astonished at his doctrine: for his word was with power.'

The first impact on his contemporaries was thus a disturbing sense of his personal authority: his power of speaking as if he knew what he was talking about, as if he had seen for himself. It was an impression he was to deepen by a variety of deeds and words. He proceeded to cure a madman, and the watchers

> were all amazed, and spake among themselves, saying, What a word is this! for with authority and power he commandeth the unclean spirits, and they come out.

Or he spoke to a man brought to him in paralysis, 'Man thy sins are forgiven thee'. And the authorities of the Jewish religion, the custodians of moral judgement, were disturbed because he thus usurped the divine authority, and they challenged his right to speak like this, until he replied by completing his word of moral healing, and curing the sick man of his paralysis. And again we

*v.18.

4

are told, 'they were all amazed.' And then he went off to dine with a despised tax-collector, a man who put the making of money before the moral and religious ideals of the nation, and who had, as such men always do, some dubious guests. And why, they asked, did Jesus join with such evil company? And his reply, independent and courageous, was returned, 'Because they are the ones I have come for. I came not to call the righteous, but sinners.'

These are the words and methods of a man who has seen something with his own eyes, and speaks from a personal conviction so intense as to amount to certainty. And in the early days this seems to have been the most noticeable thing about him: more important, surprisingly enough, than what he said. Indeed, what he said seems to have been remembered only because of this *first-hand-ness*, this quality of challenging authority. For this reason the early preaching seems almost perverse, deliberately challenging and rebellious rather than constructive. His first parable was something of a manifesto:

> No man putteth new wine into old bottles; else the new wine will burst the bottles and be spilled, and the bottles shall perish. But new wine must be put into new bottles; and both are preserved.

And he proceeds to pour his new wine into his new bottles, with a challenge to the current notions of the meaning of the Sabbath, defending the right of his followers to prepare a meal, and his own right to heal a sick man. And immediately he pressed his topsy-turvy, original thought to a rounded statement, a general challenge to all accepted opinion and all 'received' custom of thought.

> Blessed be ye poor; . . . . Blessed are ye that hunger; . . . . Blessed are ye that weep; . . . . Blessed are ye when men shall hate you; . . . .
> But woe unto you that are rich! . . . . Woe unto you that are full! . . . .
> Woe unto you that laugh! . . . . Woe unto you when all men shall speak well of you! . . . .

And then at last, after all this rebellion, comes the content of his new teaching, still aggressively, startlingly new, new bottle and new wine, but beginning to foreshadow the burden of the months to come: 'But I say unto you . . . . Love your enemies.'

This, then, is the overwhelming impression of the beginning of the ministry, that men were made breathless by the authority with which he spoke even before they had begun to understand the meaning of the words themselves. The disciples themselves were to reveal later, as they quarrelled over who should sit on the right hand of Christ in his kingdom, or as Peter drew his sword to slay a servant, that they found the lesson itself hard to learn even after they had been utterly captured by the manner of its teaching. They were first drawn to him because he spoke as if he knew, and his authority had the compelling power of first-hand conviction.

As his teaching developed, it became clear that it was a prime object of his work to help other men to see for themselves too, and to reach the same order of authoritative conviction. This impression is conveyed by two things: the close association of healing and teaching, and the method of teaching itself.

We have already seen that his healing was closely connected with his message. He assured the paralysed man that his sins were forgiven him, and restored his bodily power; and in the argument with the critics, he made plain the interdependence of the two events.* And though most accounts of the healing of the sick stop short at the physical cure, it is plain that Jesus was not himself content with mere cures. When he became famous for his power to heal, and men 'came unto him, and stayed him, that he should not depart from them', he always pressed on to other work. 'I must preach the kingdom of God to other cities also.'

But more significant even that this is the manner of the teaching itself. It is rare to have a long piece of explicit statement. Far more frequent is the parable, the story that leaves its message to be discovered, taken hold of for oneself. The gospel is full of them: set, careful vignettes like the parable of the sower, the good Samaritan, the unjust steward, the prodigal son, Dives and Lazarus, the ten pounds, and in the dark days at the end, the fig tree; or incidental parables, spontaneous similes that challenge the hearer to look for himself and see what is to be seen: the children of the bridechamber, smiting on one cheek, the blind leading the blind, the mote in a brother's eye, the children 'sitting in the market place and calling one to another and saying, We have piped unto you and ye have not danced.' This is the very idiom of his thought; and it is the idiom of a man who seeks not to impose a truth on reluctant or ignorant minds, but to awaken sleepy minds to open their eyes and look for themselves.

*When he healed the centurion's servant, he remarked on the 'faith' of the centurion; or when a woman in the crowd touched him and healed herself, he said, 'Daughter . . . . thy faith hath made thee whole'.

It is necessary to emphasize this as a corrective to a possible false interpretation of the note of authority on which we have already remarked. Men recognized his authority because he spoke with assurance; but he did not wish them to believe what he said out of deference to his authority. He wished it to 'come home' to them. The issue was squarely raised by the disciples of John the Baptist, who were sent to him to ask him to define his status: 'Art thou he that should come? or look we for another?' And Jesus replied, 'Go your way, and tell John what things ye have seen and heard.' Jesus had his startling air of authority because he, alone in his generation, spoke of what he saw. But he was working that other men should see; not that they should 'take his word for it.'

When we turn to the content of the teaching itself, we are struck at once by the absence of all systematic approach. The gospel is not itself unsystematic, but at no point is there any attempt to gather together a continuous statement of the whole truth-about-life. Jesus was clearly more concerned to illuminate a new way of looking at life, to establish a new point of view, to develop new attitudes, than to work out a system of belief and behaviour. The essence of his teaching is a new dimension rather than a complete treatment of all known dimensions. The heart of it lies in the familiar answer to the question from the lawyer, an answer which, true to his method, Jesus led the lawyer to provide himself.

> Master, what shall I do to inherit eternal life?
> He said unto him, What is written in the law? how readest thou?
> And he answering said, Thou shalt love the Lord thy God with all thy heart, and with all thy soul, and with all thy strength, and with all thy mind; and thy neighbour as thyself.

These words are so familiar now that they carry no shock of surprise: but the illustrative teaching with which Jesus sought to bring home his lesson was arresting enough in its day, and would be so today if we could look at it afresh.

'Thou shalt love the Lord thy God; and thy neighbour as thyself.' What does it *mean*? It means that we learn to transfer to all men something of the sense of caring for, of being involved with, of responsibility for those whom we have lived among and learnt to love.

'Thy mother and thy brethren stand without, desiring to see thee,' said some in the crowd. 'My mother and my brethren are these which hear the word of God, and do it,' said Jesus in reply.

Or the elder brother spoke, expressing the world's view of the meaning of love in the words,

> Lo, these many years do I serve thee, neither transgressed I at any time thy commandment: and yet thou never gavest me a kid, that I might make merry with my friends: but as soon as this thy son was come, which hath devoured thy living with harlots, thou hast killed for him the fatted calf.

And the father, loving with this new kind of love, returned,

> It was meet that we should make merry and be glad: for this thy brother was dead, and is alive again; and was lost and is found.

Or his disciples responded to a situation with the old, normal, 'human' responses, and would call down fire from heaven on a village that would not take him in; and Jesus replied,

> Ye know not what manner of spirit ye are of. For the Son of man is not come to destroy men's lives, but to save them.

And he chose one of the same Samaritans who had thus rejected him to be the hero of one of his parables, to illustrate the nature of this new love that transcends the daily, common thing that we know.

This new love is not a 'feeling for', but a 'feeling with'; not an attraction towards, but a sharing of a point of view; an understanding of what it is like to *be* the object of it, an insight into the inward condition of a runaway son or a lost sheep or a battered wreck by the roadside or a member of a village community who are afraid to welcome Jesus 'because his face was as though he would go to Jerusalem'; or indeed to be in any need. Jesus drew continuously on the metaphor of fatherhood, as the nearest thing to what he was seeking to illuminate. To a father children matter in proportion as they need him. The child who grows up straight, strong and joyous is a source of delight; but it is the child who is burdened and crooked and maladjusted who *costs* the father most, who *matters* most, whom he carries about in his heart when he goes about his other business. It is the black sheep whom he *prays for*. And as that is true of fatherhood at its best, it is also true of the divine family. As we learn to love like God, we learn to love all people in this way, and to weigh people up, as it were, not in terms of what they can give us but of what we can give them, to assess them in terms of need rather than strength.

With this as his central message, it is easy to see why Jesus laid such emphasis on first-hand experience. We cannot love to order, and no moral imperative, however weighty, will enable us to know what it is like to be someone else in need. It is for this reason that he found it necessary to issue a set challenge to the Pharisaic way of thinking. The Pharisees were not men who did harm; but their whole approach to life would prevent good, for it prevented the inward apprehension, the personal insight, which was what mattered. And so Jesus denounced them:

> Now do ye Pharisees make clean the outside of the cup and the platter, but your inward part is full of ravening and wickedness . . . . Woe unto you, Pharisees! for ye tithe mint and rue and all manner of herbs, and pass over judgement and the love of God : . . . . Woe unto you, scribes and Pharisees, hypocrites! for ye are as graves which appear not, and the men that walk over them are not aware of them.

Loving, it is plain, does not mean indulgence. It means a concern for another person's true interest; and the trouble with the Pharisees was that they felt no sense of need. They thought all was well with them; and in thinking so they misled their people. Those to whom Jesus was tender, 'loving' in the common sense of the word, were those despised, hurt people who knew their own weakness, who knew that they needed help.

This would be the basis of the Christian account of man, if we were to press the teaching of Jesus on to the system that he never himself defined : the claim that man cannot grow until he is made aware of his need. The truth about humanity is its dependence, the continuance after childhood of the same conditions of growth. As soon as we think we can 'bring ourselves up', we lose the power to be brought up.

> Whosoever exalteth himself shall be abased; and he that humbleth himself shall be exalted.
> Whosoever shall seek to save his life shall lose it; and whosoever shall lose his life shall preserve it.

This doctrine of dependence has often been narrowed in Christian apologetic to the moral sphere, and it has been claimed that we cannot behave well 'by ourselves', but need a special measure of grace to recover from the results of previous failure. There is a certain psychological justification for this argument, in that neurotics think so much of themselves that they cannot escape from the imprisonment of their own failure; but when Jesus described the dependence of man he was illustrating a truth much less debatable than this highly controversial, and not very important, matter of how far we can 'save' ourselves morally by our own efforts. He was claiming that man is only man in so far as he recognizes his dependence, his interdependence with other men. Man is meant to be a lover, and he cannot be a lover unless there are men to love. Sin is all that impedes our loving and understanding each other – and that is why pride is graver than vagabondage, complacency more dangerous than cowardice. Self-reliance, independence, isolation, withdrawal – these are the attitudes that cause spiritual decay. They are dangerous, like the faults of the Pharisees, because they can be made to appear like virtues. Independence has a fine sturdy ring about it; but it is the enemy of interdependence.

But how is this interdependence to be learnt? How can men come to love one another, when they are so often unlovely? It is here that the teaching and work of Christ reach down to the central issues. Other teachers have said something after the manner of what I have just outlined; but here, in his answer to this question, Jesus takes on the unique quality which all interpretations of him have found it impossible to ignore. For more than any other teacher, he made plain that this was no mere speculative position, no mere intellectual and æsthetic statement of what it is desirable that men should believe. He laid emphasis in words, and finally by flinging his life into the scale, on the supreme claim that all this was a truth-of-life, and not merely a truth-of-thought. The only way to grasp it is to live it: we cannot do it by surveying the field of intellectual and moral problems, and taking up an attitude, or embracing a belief. The ordinary modes of behaviour, based on common-sense self-interest, need radical overturning.

> Take no thought for your life, what ye shall eat; neither for the body, what ye shall put on . . . . But rather seek ye the kingdom of God; and all these things shall be added unto you . . . . Sell that ye have, and give alms; provide yourselves bags which wax not old, a treasure in the heavens that faileth not, where no thief approacheth, neither moth corrupteth.

The normally accepted objects of life, comfort, prestige, security, are here declared to be irrelevant, dangerous indeed, hurtful to the true objects of life. It is spiritual value for which we live; or, if we do not, we miss life itself. We must be *committed*. The lesson is pressed home time and again.

Whosoever he be of you that forsaketh not all that he hath, he cannot be my disciple.

No servant can serve two masters: for either he will hate the one, and love the other; or else he will hold to the one, and despise the other. Ye cannot serve God and mammon.

There are those who would argue that this call for complete dedication of life and goods was meant only for his immediate followers, the handful who had a specially urgent task in world evangelism, no longer applicable now that the Christian witness is better organized; but Peter asked this very question, 'Lord, speakest thou this parable unto us, or even to all?', and received the reply that any servant guarding his master's house must live by the rules of the absent owner.

But and if that servant say in his heart, My lord delayeth his coming; and shall begin to beat the menservants and maidens, and to eat and drink, and to be drunken; the lord of that servant will come in a day when he looketh not for him, and at an hour when he is not aware, and will cut him in sunder, and will appoint him his portion with the unbelievers.

This image of the servants, and the house, and the absent owner is fundamental to the view of the world and reality that lay behind the teaching of Jesus. The world *looks* as if it is handed over to humanity, with its virtues and vices, its need of wealth and force and cunning and bodily comfort and rank and prestige; but in reality this is the illusion. The truth is that the world is waiting for its master, owned by a God of love whose eternal values find no room for these human ways of thought, but who demands instead poverty, and meekness and simplicity and integrity and humility. This God is 'absent', not immediately apparent to the eye of the body or mind; but it is his world; and if, because he seems not to be there, men begin to 'beat the menservants and maidens, and to eat and drink, and to be drunken', then they betray their trust. 'And unto whomsoever much is given, of him shall much be required.' Repeatedly it is made clear, whether in these explicit revolutions of conventional thought, or in some mere trick of metaphor, that Jesus was wholly and unquestionably sure of God.

Thou shalt worship the Lord thy God, and him only shalt thou serve.
How is it that ye sought me? wist ye not that I must be about my Father's business?
Fear not, little flock; for it is the Father's good pleasure to give you the kingdom.

Father, if thou be willing, remove this cup from me: nevertheless, not my will, but thine, be done.

The whole mode of his thought and speech is determined by this assumption of God's point of view. In any one else, this kind of language would be arrogance; to his enemies it was blasphemy: but to those who are 'reached' by it, it seems merely inevitable.

It was this clear-eyed wholeness of dependence on God that led him, in the end, to the Cross. Humanly speaking there was no reason for it. He might have lived honourably and beneficently, healing the minds and bodies of men, but he rejected that easy way, easy for him and for those whom he would benefit. 'Man shall not live by bread alone.' Or he could have made a bid for political power (and the Jewish revolt in A.D. 70 came near enough to success to suggest that Jesus might have had a genuine opportunity of triumph; if not, perhaps, of overthrowing the empire, at least of establishing a Kingdom of the Jews which Rome would accept as autonomous in all except a few issues of international relationships); but he rejected this too: 'Thou shalt worship the Lord thy God, and him only shalt thou serve.' Or he could have withdrawn into an eminence of magic prestige, the wonder-worker of his day, performing miracles that should magnify his own fame; but this would have been to deny his whole vision of the supremacy of God: 'Thou shalt not tempt the Lord thy God.' And though the story of the temptations occurs at the beginning of the gospel narrative, and as time went on Jesus was to some extent committed to a position which the Jews must have found disturbing, it was never too late to take one of these alternative lines of action. His disciples did not realize that he was treading a more dangerous way until the tragedy was upon them, and his warnings were ignored:

The Son of man shall be delivered into the hands of men. But they understood not this saying, and it was hid from them.

And on Palm Sunday it must have seemed to them that Jesus was about to take possession of a kingdom that was rightly his; and a significant exchange with the Pharisees reveals that to Jesus, at least, the way was clearly open had he wanted it. The Pharisees were angry because his disciples had shouted their triumph, proclaiming 'the King that cometh in the name of the Lord.' 'Master,' said the Pharisees, 'rebuke thy disciples.'

And he answered and said unto them, I tell you that, if these should hold their peace, the stones would immediately cry out.

Had he wished to mobilize popular feeling, he had the power and the occasion to do it. The Jewish leaders themselves would soon have been behind him, and he could have hoped, reasonably, to establish the lost glories of Judaism in all the spiritual atmosphere of a theocracy. It was no ignoble end, this; but Jesus turned away from it to march to Calvary.

He has left us no explanation of his motive in thus accepting what would seem to be defeat. He left this supreme moment, as he left so much, for us to see for ourselves. The message is too deep for words, or systems of belief or interpretations, or the gloss of comment. Men have sought to supply the gloss, but every generation has seen something different in its meaning; and one age has revolted from the comment of another.

One thing is clear: the story of the cross is bound to the whole message and life of Jesus. The complete opposition between conventional ways of thought and the assumption of God's point of view is summed up in death that is accepted instead of avoided. Looking at life 'from the other side' involves the reversal of our usual hopes and fears and intentions: and at the point of death the two sides are both to be seen at once, their difference starting here. All human ideals, however they differ in detail — the varied faiths and creeds that men have evolved — agree in this, that death is the ultimate tragedy. They differ on what is good and what bad, but death is the end because it reduces good and bad to nothing. But to Jesus, seeing, as it were, with the eyes of God, death was merely a denial of the transitory: it was a mere incident in eternity. God and man's life in God continued uninterrupted by death: it is only man, and man's life in himself, that come to an end.

The form of the death served to heighten this great symbolism of the supreme choice. It was shameful — and the shame of it would strike a contemporary more than the physical agony; it was a public display of the emptying, stripping and denigrating of human personality. The little rags of human prestige were torn away, and the body of the criminal was shown to the world, crushed, insignificant, nothing.

This emptying of himself Jesus chose as the climax of his work: filling a human life with glory by first emptying it of all that men thought of as glory. He claimed his supremacy by standing last, laid hold of his title by casting everything away. And the first recognition of what he had done came as he died, from a Roman soldier standing by the cross: 'Certainly this was a righteous man', or, in the other gospels, 'Truly, this was the Son of God'. Here, as he died in peace, accepting what men did to him not only willingly but lovingly, was a man so filled with a spirit beyond human capacity for greatness that there was no escape from this recognition of God in him. It was the first assertion of the divinity of Christ.

Later, the Church was to press this same concept of the divinity of Christ to the centre of its thinking, and build upon it an intellectual framework of immense complexity. In a sense this is necessary for intellectual integrity; in another sense it is misleading, for it has come to carry a meaning separated from the fact itself, like the fanciful message of a piece of music. But there is no meaning in the doctrine of the divinity of Christ unless this be at its heart: that the sacrifice of his life, in such loving willingness, should be seen to be so overwhelmingly complete and inevitable that we cannot escape the conclusion that this is the work of God. It is either illusion or deity; less than human or more than human; folly or a wisdom that man does not make by himself. And to claim Jesus as divine is not, in the first place, to make metaphysical distinctions or claims about his personal relationship with the creator, but simply to respond as the soldier responded, with a humble recognition of something final, something that by its own virtue will last beyond the discovery of the emptiness and transience of human desires.

But it was not merely that, not simply the denial of ordinary human valuations. That is what suicide is, the assertion that contrary to belief, life is not worth living. Jesus, in his acceptance of suffering and death, made no suggestion that life was not worth living: he claimed that life was of a value beyond itself, that man fulfils himself as he is expended and used, that the seed grows only if it is hidden in the ground, and that 'he that loseth his life shall find it'. We should normally expect to regard death as the end, and men would be forgiven if, under the threat of death, they thought of themselves and their own safety. But to Jesus death was the supreme opportunity of demonstrating in action the law of love, the law that man does not live to himself alone but to others, and that he is most valuable when he is wasted and squandered for another's good.

Even in this moment of his final sacrifice, his disciples were still
blind to this truth. When it was all over, they were to share their
grief with the stranger on the Emmaus road, lamenting the
'prophet mighty in deed and word', whose death had robbed
them of their hope:

> We trusted that it had been he which should have redeemed Israel.

And the stranger reproved them for their slowness of heart and
lack of insight:

> Ought not Christ to have suffered these things and to have entered into
> his glory?

It was all one to Jesus, the suffering and the glory. He could not
show how far love could go without going the uttermost distance.
It had to be *done*, not only talked about.

Men have recognized this necessity for achievement in deed by
the formulation of the doctrine of the atonement, at some periods
a strange, indeed monstrous, doctrine; at others more gracious,
less legalistic, but mystical and intangible; but the doctrine has
haunted Christian thought, for in some inexplicable way the death
of Christ seems to have *done* something. Humanity, in the human
figure of Jesus, has once and for all moved out of its security and
selfishness and defensiveness to the limit of experience, and has
stood in the darkest depths and become one with God. It is in
selflessness and love that man is made at one with the divine
purpose that sustains the world; and in perfect selflessness and
love, in the conditions most hostile to it, that man becomes
perfectly at one with the divine. Love chooses of set purpose
the environment in which it has nothing to feed on that it might
have the more to give.

> If ye love them which love you, what thank have ye? for sinners also
> love those that love them. And if ye do good to them which do good to
> you, what thank have ye? for sinners also do even the same . . But love
> ye your enemies and do good, and lend, hoping for nothing again; and
> your reward shall be great, and ye shall be the children of the Highest;
> for he is kind unto the unthankful and to the evil.

And it is with the finality of the ultimate sacrifice that this theme
is taken up with the work of love on the Cross: the self-
forgetfulness of the comfort to the daughters of Jerusalem:
'Weep not for me, but weep for yourselves.' Or the positive,
creative love leaping across to the murderers: 'Father forgive

hem, for they know not what they do.' Or the final assertion of
unity with the God who had thus let him die: 'Father, into thy
hands I commend my spirit.'

This death was not the end. The disciples thought it was, and
they shrank back from the last hour in black despair. But in
strange ways they found that despair was the wrong response. As
Jesus had led humanity to the limit of its destiny, so he had led
it to the point where God could begin to use it in a way that
transcended previous experience. We are so far away from these
events in time, and, more important, in spiritual insight, that we
cannot 'explain' what happened next. But in any case, 'explanation' is irrelevant: explanation is merely the description of an
event in terms of normally accepted categories of thought and
experience; and it is beyond doubt that the entire human and
spiritual situation at this time transcended normal categories.
What is certain, is that his disciples received unshakable, overwhelming assurance that as Jesus in his death reversed the current
human values, he released into human experience hitherto
unsuspected powers of the spirit. He had become at one with
God; and had set free the spirit of God to work upon humanity
in a totally new way. And so his followers stumbled upon the
truth which was to send them travelling the highways of the
Roman empire, the conviction that Jesus, whom they had known
in the flesh, had risen from the tomb and was alive in God.

This was the achieved purpose of his life and death, that mankind should have before it an inescapable expression of the reality
of spiritual values. The things of God are not a matter of taste
or whim or individual choice, like a hobby or a form of art: they
are the things that the universe is made of and that man is made
for: as the beauty of a symphony is not something you can take
or leave, using the sounds by themselves for some purpose of your
own. The beauty is the thing the sounds are there to make; and it
is equally no matter of indifference that men should take what
sounds they please from the harmonies of the universe. It is the
music that is real, and the sounds insignificant unless they carry
the deeper meaning. The message of Jesus is that the universe
is no neutral territory in which man can wander at will and see
what he can make of himself, with nobody to mind much what it
is, except man himself. He asserted, in his teaching and loving
and above all in this tremendous impact of his spirit beyond
death, that the universe was on a particular side, built out of

chaos and sustained in time to this very end, that men should learn to be used by a loving purpose.

Can this be true? We have seen that reason, in its modern idiom of the scientific method, falls short of certainty, and can answer neither yes nor no. If we ponder the story of human thought in previous ages we shall see that the same is true of reason in the idiom of other times: we cannot 'prove' the existence of God, nor prove his non-existence. But one unshakable fact remains since Jesus wrote his message upon history: the fact that *he* was true. And while metaphysic still remains, despite the spread of education, a specialist affair that most men can live without, no man can live without a personal judgement, in terms of deeds and daily choices, of living and loving and hating, about the meaning of human personality. Jesus appeals to men as the supreme interpretation of humanity, and the challenge he makes is to force upon us the choice between regarding him as a freak, a sport, a chance by-product of a union of cultures, or as the man who fulfilled the purposes of God.

This choice is not primarily an intellectual matter, though the intellect plays its part, as the optic nerve plays its part in our response to a picture. But as our whole personality is involved in our response to great art, so is our whole personality called upon by the challenge of Christ. If we choose to ignore him, we choose to rob mankind of the significance he gave it; if we find we cannot ignore him, we are driven on to the point where we are ourselves involved in the same purposes, and as he was used, we find ourselves used too, by the same living power. In the making of the choice, Christians have used the word 'faith'. There is no final evidence, and we must choose by faith, they have said. So much of medieval Christian dogma, which was also accepted by faith, has been exploded that the very word is discredited, and faith has come to mean for most men the blind acceptance of what other men think it is good for us to believe.

In truth, as we have seen, we live in all that matters by probabilities, by the choice of what, when all is taken into account, appeals to us as something that ought to be true. Faith has been defined by Dean Inge as 'the resolution to stand or fall by the noblest hypothesis', and it is that kind of faith that reaches out to Christ. There is no great resolution required in seeing Jesus as the noblest of men: but there is much in standing by the hypothesis that Jesus represents what God would make of men;

and the further faith that God has not left man to make himself, but is himself active in his own purposes. Yet can we accept one without the other? It seems surely improbable, to say the least, that Jesus achieved the height of human understanding while being utterly wrong in his belief about God. It is improbable that a life that imported a new vision of truth into human life should yet have been based on a lie, or that a life that, merely to read of it, sets men's hearts thrilling with a new meaning, should itself be contradictory and meaningless. They do no service to the cause of Christianity who deny that there are difficulties in accepting or even understanding every aspect of the gospel narrative; but though inaccuracies, exaggerations, distortions or plain illusions may have affected the narrative of certain episodes, nothing seriously affects the clear picture of a life and death that speak of the eternal breaking into human life. Whom say ye that I am? said Jesus to his disciples. And Peter answered, for himself and for countless men and women who have seen something of what he saw, 'The Christ of God.'

CHAPTER FIVE

'Primitive Christianity Revived'

WHEN the Quaker movement arose, in the middle of the seventeenth century, organized Christianity seemed to be breaking down. The early followers of Jesus had suffered and loved as had Jesus himself, and a new concept of human life had slowly reached out across the world. In the fullness of time, it had conquered the seats of the mighty, and the Roman emperor had declared himself a Christian; and the life of the early church had been subtly changed to suit the altered circumstances. Still exercising a profound influence for good, the ideal of love had been adapted to the responsibilities of power. Popes arose who sought to increase the secular power of the church in order that the spiritual power of the church might be advanced, and the strong arm was used to enforce morality. For a time the Christian ideal, in its new adaptation, was supreme in the western world, and the power of the church was secure in the moral sphere and in the political and economic structure which sustained life.

But the whole method of maintaining this supremacy was doomed, and the attacks of science on dogma, of individuals on obedience to an imposed moral code, of nationalism on the unity imposed by the church, and of personal religious experience on the hierachic system of the Roman church all combined to produce the complex series of events we lump together under the title of the Reformation. The years during which these changes were taking place were years of suffering and bitter cruelty that increasingly denied the Christianity they were supposed to promote; until by the middle of the seventeenth century it seemed the end had been reached. The phase of violent and frequent martyrdom had seemed to be over, but the same spirit welled up in the Civil War and its cruel end, when a king was executed by men who believed themselves the specially appointed agents of divine justice. These men, for the moment in the seat of power, were pledged to the suppression of gaiety and lightness of heart and their replacement by earnest moral endeavour and a spiritual uniformity none the less stringent for passing under the title of Independent. It was at precisely this moment of the king's execution, that George Fox, the son of a Leicestershire weaver, was impelled to burst into a church in Nottingham, a 'great steeplehouse', as he called it, and protest aloud against the sermon. He describes the scene in his journal in these words:

> All the people looked like fallow ground and the priest, like a great lump of earth, stood in his pulpit above. He took for his text these words of Peter, 'We have also a more sure word of prophecy whereunto ye do well that ye take heed, as unto a light that shineth in a dark place until the day dawn, and the day star arise in your hearts'. And he told the people that this was the Scriptures, by which they were to try all doctrines, religions, and opinions. Now the Lord's power was so mighty upon me and so strong in me, that I could not hold, but was made to cry out and say, 'O no, it is not the Scriptures', and I told them what it was, namely, the Holy Spirit, by which the holy men of God gave forth the Scriptures, whereby opinions, religions, and judgements were to be tried; for it led into all truth, and so gave the knowledge of all truth. The Jews had the Scriptures and yet resisted the Holy Ghost, and rejected Christ, the bright morning star. They persecuted Christ and His apostles, and took upon them to try their doctrines by the Scriptures, but erred in judgement, and did not try them aright, because they tried without the Holy Ghost.

In this, his first public utterance, Fox fastened on what was to be the supreme issue between Quakers and other Christians, the question of authority. It was inherent in the historical situation. The Roman church had held undisputed power for hundreds of years, undisputed in its fundamentals, however different kings and emperors might have disputed the frontier between spiritual and secular power. But with Wyclif, Luther and the other reformers the authority of the church was called into question. In place of the church, speaking through its human organization of pope and cardinal and priest, they erected the authority of the Bible, now translated into the vernacular and available for all literate men to read for themselves. Here was an authority that could not be corrupted by selfishness or greed or lust, as a priest could; here was the voice of God, written for all time, unchangeable, unequivocal, unchallengeable. It was along these lines that the fundamental argument between the reformers and the old church was conducted, and the sermon that Fox found himself listening to was thus a conventional statement of the central issue.

But to Fox it appeared that the whole debate was irrelevant.

5

He had already been brought violently to the knowledge that the Scriptures did not by themselves make Christian men, when he had joined two Puritan friends in a glass of beer.

> When we had drunk a glass apiece they began to drink healths, calling for more, and agreeing together that he that would not drink should pay all. I was grieved that any who made profession of religion should do so . . . wherefore I rose up to be gone, and putting my hand into my pocket, laid a groat on the table before them, and said, 'If it be so, I'll leave you.'

From this experience he began to exercise his mind with the problem of authority, concluding that it was not conferred by education, and 'that being bred at Oxford or Cambridge was not enough to fit and qualify men to be ministers of Christ'; nor was it connected with sacred buildings, though

> both priests and people used to call their temples or churches dreadful places, holy ground, and the temples of God. But the Lord shewed me, so that I did see clearly that He did not dwell in these temples which men had commanded and set up, but in people's hearts.

In this way, one after another of the recognized religious authorities seemed to fail him, until he withdrew from all the quarrelling groups.

> As I had forsaken the priests, so I left the Separate preachers also, and those called the most experienced people; for I saw there was none among them all that could speak to my condition. And when all my hopes in them and in all men were gone, so that I had nothing outwardly to help me, nor could I tell what to do; then, oh! then I heard a voice which said, 'There is one, even Christ Jesus, that can speak to thy condition', and when I heard it, my heart did leap for joy.

He had found his authority in the living voice of Christ, as Christ himself had found his authority in the living voice of God. This was to become the central principle of Quakerism, the key to all the rest.

There is a certain inevitability about its discovery at precisely this moment in time. Men were tiring (though the grim events of the next few years were to show that they were not yet tired enough) of attempting to settle the dispute over authority by the appeal to force. One side could burn the leaders of the other side, and the other side could have its revenge: but that settled nothing. One side could gain political power, and the other could struggle to recover it. But even that settled nothing. Where was the impartial umpire to decide the issue? A government could decide which should prevail for the time, but not which *ought* to prevail. And the two rival authorities themselves seemed to depend on each other. The Bible told the story of the events that led to the founding of the church, and so would seem to claim priority. But the Bible was written by the church, and was thus a document created by the prior authority of the living community.

The temper of the age, empirical and scientific, pointed to individual choice as the answer to this dilemma, each man for himself choosing the authority he would accept. But this was not entirely satisfactory, for if that were accepted it would in the end destroy authority altogether. An authority that a man chooses for himself is in the end no authority at all. And thus the way would be open to whims and eccentricities of all sorts, as Fox himself found while travelling on his own quest, meeting one group arguing that 'women have no souls . . . . no more than a goose,' or another people 'that relied much on dreams'.

When Fox recognized the only authority as that of 'one, even Christ Jesus' he was taking up a very different attitude from these individualists: he was turning to the life of Jesus himself, perceiving his dependence on a living contact with God, and claiming that the object of his life had been that men should see for themselves the meaning of the divine love. He was taking seriously the whole message of Christ. Men were not left, he claimed, to the guidance of a church administered by evil men; nor were they entrusted to a book, in the interpretation of which whimsy could play as decisive a part as in any moral judgement. On the contrary, men were given a power of spiritual insight which should enable them to know for themselves what the Scriptures were about: they should know the truths that set the evangelists writing. They thus had power to *judge* the Scriptures by the light which the Scriptures reflect. As a Friend was later to put it,

> We can truly say concerning the Scriptures, that now we believe not so much because of the relation of things concerning Christ which we have found in them, but because we have seen and received the thing which the Scriptures speak of.[*]

This would seem to offer no guarantee against the folly of eccentric originality, and that is the heavy truth, that it does, indeed, offer no guarantee. But nor does the use of the Bible as the authority, for there is so much to interpret in its narrative

[*]Isaac Penington: *A Question to the Professors of Christianity.*

and moral injunction that ignorance and pride can do as much harm with the Bible to aid them as they can by themselves. And the authority of the living church, with its bishops and priests, though less liable to mere whimsy, is still susceptible to pride and ignorance. There is no way of making quite certain that human beings will avoid error except to put them to death.

But though that is true, it does not mean that men are utterly at the mercy of pride and ignorance. Man must seek the highest he can reach, not merely seek to defend himself from the worst that can befall. and the highest is this gift of divine insight, the power of seeing for himself what God has sought to reveal. Perhaps this is best described as a power of *recognition*, the capacity to know the truth when we meet it, and thus to find in the Scriptures or in the world that which we have been created to see.

It was because Fox came when he did that the argument centred upon the authority of the Scriptures. A hundred years earlier he would have been more concerned with the priesthood. It was a necessary corollary of this belief in the inward apprehension of the life of Christ that when Fox gathered round himself a number of kindred spirits, seekers of first hand-experience, they should find themselves able to dispense with an ordained priesthood. Indeed, for the first few years they had practically no organization at all; and when they increased sufficiently in number to need administration, the system was carefully designed to emphasize the priesthood of all believers, and the responsibility of each individual member, not only for his work in the community, but for his own grasp of the truth. Any member of the church might thus be led to preach the gospel, and he would be listened to in the same spirit as the Bible was read, in the hope of being 'recognized' as the bearer of the truth. Even women were thus heard, and through the whole history of Quakerism there has been no significant difference between the rôle of men and women in the work of the society.

The liberty laid upon all members to follow the light as they saw it led, inevitably, to excesses, and Fox was compelled to turn his attention to the problem of organization, the details of which will be considered later; but at no time has the society departed from this insight achieved at the outset, in the rejection of the safeguards of priest and book, and the bold committal of the whole enterprise to the living guidance of the spirit of Christ.

And as the early 'Friends of Truth', as they began to call them-selves, came to regard the two rival sources of authority as inadequate, they found they could also dispense with the rival forms of worship. The sects were quarrelling over the number of sacraments, or the place of music in worship, or the garments of the priest; but Friends gathered in silence and were found of God without any of these things. Alexander Parker described the mode of worship thus:

> The first that enters into the place of your Meeting, turn in thy mind and wait upon God singly, as if none were present but the Lord . . . Then the next that comes in, let them in simplicity of heart sit down and turn in to the same light, and wait in the spirit; and so all the rest coming in, in the fear of the Lord, sit down in pure stillness and silence of all flesh, and wait in the light. Those who are brought to a pure, still waiting upon God in the spirit are come nearer to the Lord than words are: for God is a Spirit, and in the spirit is He worshipped. In such a meeting there will be an unwillingness to part asunder, being ready to say in yourselves, it is good to be here; this is the end of words and writings—to bring people to the eternal living word.°

There was thus no argument as to the correct form to use in the worship of God: God provided his own form for men who turned towards him in silence. 'The pure motions and breathings of God's Spirit are felt to arise,' wrote Robert Barclay,** 'from which, as words of declaration, prayers or praises arise, the acceptable worship is known, which edifies the church, and is well pleasing to God. And no man here limits the Spirit of God, nor brings forth his own conned and gathered stuff; but every one puts that forth which the Lord puts into their hearts: and it is uttered forth not in man's will and wisdom, but in the evidence and demonstration of the Spirit, and of power.'

And as they thus denied the necessity of forms of worship, they denied also the necessity of sacramental rites. A man became a Christian by learning to love God as he had learnt to see him in Christ, not by being touched with water from the font. He was sustained in his Christian life by the food of love in the heart, not by the bread and wine on the altar. A modern statement of the Quaker attitude on these matters would say, 'There is no harm in the outward rites: all that matters is the inward meaning they symbolize.' But to the early Friends there *was* harm in the outward rites, for they were a cause of strife between Christians.

In Pure Stillness and Silence of all flesh.
°°*Apology.*

It is important to remember this historic situation, for otherwise the Quaker position seems merely negative, casting away a symbol while agreeing with traditional Christianity in valuing the thing symbolized. But they were convinced that the over-attention to the symbol was denying the truth itself: that men were washing in physical water and forgetting the harder task of cleansing in the spirit; that they were feeding on bread and wine, and failing to make the greater effort to 'draw near in faith' and 'feed on him' in the heart. What mattered in worship was not what seemed to be happening in the outward show of word and ritual, but what was really happening in the hearts of the worshippers.

> Yea, though there be not a word spoken, yet is the true spiritual worship performed, and the body of Christ edified; yea, it may, and hath often fallen out among us, that divers meetings have passed without one word; and yet our souls have been greatly edified and refreshed, and our hearts wonderfully overcome with the secret sense of God's power and Spirit, which without words have been ministered from one vessel to another.*

This same attitude, of paying more attention to the reality of the inward experience than to the outward formulation of it, led to a suspicion of the whole business of theology, from which the Society has but recently recovered, and the effects of which can still be seen. Theology was suspect because, like ritual, it was a matter for dispute between Christians. Men were killing each other because of their beliefs, and heresy was more serious than vice. But to early Friends, theology was not important enough, or sure enough, to cause such strife. In a controversial pamphlet William Penn put the typical Quaker view in these words:

> It is not opinion, or speculation, or notions of what is true; or assent to, or the subscription of, articles or propositions, though never so soundly worded, that makes a man a true believer or a true Christian. But it is conformity of mind and practice to the will of God, in all holiness of conversation, according to the dictates of the divine principle of light and life in the soul, which denotes a person truly a child of God.

'It is not . . . . notions.' And it was as 'notions' that Friends were to attack theological speculation for generations.

These different aspects of the early Quaker emphasis are all parts of one fundamental: that the true Christian is one who grows like Christ from within, not one who takes up a particular moral or sectarian position. In claiming this to be the mark of the

*Barclay, op. cit.

Christian way, they were seeking to interpret the work of Jesus himself, who had directed men's attention from the outward form to the inward meaning. And it was because of this that the early Friends felt able to claim that Quakerism was 'primitive Christianity revived', representing their search as an attempt to look where Christ had enjoined us to look. They saw in his response to the decadence of Jewish religion a guide to them as they came face to face with a decadent Christian religion; and they took, as literal truth, all he had said of the way men could learn of God in their own lives. Like their contemporaries, they were skilled in the use of biblical quotation, and their apologetic is full of references to the New Testament which illustrate the earnestness of their desire to be 'lived in' by the spirit of Christ as Christ himself was 'lived in' by God.

They thus came to regard the crucifixion less as a work of atonement, achieved by Jesus for all time on our behalf, than as an expression of an attitude to mankind, achieved by Jesus that it might be achieved also by his followers. He had taught men the meaning of the love of God by suffering, and continuing to love through the suffering. His followers had sought to teach the love of God by compulsion, the suppression of heresy and the punishment of sin. The early Friends set about proclaiming their message by word of mouth and by the loving contact of personality, rejecting any possibility of the use of force. This was at the time an issue which called for decision from every man who sought to express his beliefs in action, and the leaders of the sects called on their followers to take up arms in defence of the truth. Before Quakerism was an organized community, there were thus men who, struggling to live after the law of Christ, found themselves impelled to put away the sword. One of these was William Dewsbury:

> I joined with that little remnant which said they fought for the gospel, but I found no rest to my soul amongst them. And the word of the Lord came unto me and said, 'Put up thy sword into thy scabbard; if my kingdom were of this world, then would my children fight', which word enlightened my heart and discovered the mystery of iniquity, and that the Kingdom of Christ was within, and the enemies was within, and was spiritual, and my weapons against them must be spiritual, the power of God.*

And when George Fox himself was called upon to fight for the Commonwealth against the king, he replied:

*The discovery of the great enmity of the serpent.

I told them I knew from whence all wars arose, even from the lust . . . and that I lived in the virtue of that life and power that took away the occasion of all wars.

The spread of the gospel was to rely, they believed, on peaceful persuasion, and the appeal of love and the might of a living truth. And thus rejecting the outward values of force and physical authority, they also rejected the values of prestige and rank. In the first instance this was not a fully developed theory of social justice, but a concrete, vivid reaction against the artificial distinctions between men current at the time. Manners were elaborate, so Quakers dispensed with manners. Costume was elaborate, so Quakers dressed with the utmost austerity. Speech had its distinctions, so Quakers changed their habits of speech.

This last is perhaps the Quaker peculiarity best known outside the society. It was the custom to address as 'you' anyone whom one wished to honour, a superior or an equal in rank. 'Thou' was reserved for servants, the lower orders, and for intimate friends. Time has solved the problem by making us use 'you' to all men, but the early Quaker was driven to use 'thou' to them all. 'I was required,' says Fox, 'to Thee and Thou all men and women, without any respect to rich or poor, great or small. And as I travelled up and down, I was not to bid people Good morrow or Good evening; neither might I bow or scrape with my leg to any one.'

These seem trivial points to the looker on, but to Friends they were far from trivial. They looked to the *meaning* of the trivial, when other men would argue that the thing in itself was so small that its meaning could be ignored. These things *mattered,* they insisted; and they were so emphatic in their literal obedience to what they saw that they were, in the words of Penn,

> like men . . . upon whom the ends of the world were come . . . Now this I say, and that in the fear and presence of the all-seeing, just God, the present honour and respect of the world, among other things, became burdensome to us: we saw they had no being in paradise, that they grew in the night-time, and came from an ill root; and that they only delighted a vain and ill mind, and that much pride and folly were in them.°

They were trying to live as if it were true that the spiritual world were more real than the material world: and if that led to strange

°*No cross, no crown.*

topsy-turviness in some of their conduct, they had good precedent for it: 'We shall easily grant,' Penn continues,

> our honour, as our religion, is more hidden; and that neither are so discernible by worldly men, nor grateful to them. Our plainness is odd, uncouth, and goes mightily against the grain; but so does Christianity too, and that for the same reasons.

If the early Friend seemed a blunt, unresponsive man, it was because he was seeking to respond only to the voice of God within him.

As would be expected, these people ran into trouble, with their root-and-branch insistence on inward experience, their denial of the importance of what other Christians were most concerned to defend, and the extreme oddity of their social behaviour. They were arrested for failing to pay tithes, which they objected to because they disapproved of a hireling ministry. They were arrested too for disturbing public worship, since other Friends followed Fox's example in expressing their horror at the preacher's message. It was a custom of the time to discuss the sermon after it was over, but Friends could not wait so long, and denounced the preacher roundly. This, in a day when forms of worship were the focal point of the whole complex dispute, was serious enough; but when Friends arrived in court they stirred up the animosity of magistrates and justices by refusing to take the oath, or to remove their hats. The oath was objectionable because it implied that a man was expected to be untruthful when not on oath; and Friends asserted the necessity of utter integrity in daily life to the point of refusing to draw any distinction between the sacramental truth of the courts and the plain truth of honest dealing. Their hats they would not remove because they could not show to men the reverence they kept for God. Their 'theeing and thouing', a part of the same witness to the equality of all men in the sight of God, annoyed the magistrates further, and Friends brought down on their heads a virulence and exaggeration in the administration of justice out of all proportion to the offences.

The offences themselves, of course, were not the whole story. It was a troubled age, with the memory of a long and bitter war, and the death of a king still fresh in men's minds. Quakers, who seemed to go out of their way to deny the authority of magistrates, seemed more like anarchists than peaceful citizens, and they appealed unintentionally to the deep, unreasoning fear that operates so powerfully below the surface. The Quakers were seeking to assert the rule of God; but they seemed to be merely denying the rule of man. And in those days, as indeed in any day, a belief that seems to threaten the essential framework of order on which we depend for the bare means of livelihood calls up a fierce and unrelenting spirit. They were thus imprisoned in large numbers; and when in prison they refused to bribe their way to the little comfort that might ensure survival, and many of them died in prison. Even if they did try to protect themselves a little, their angry gaolers made them rue it. Fox's account of his imprisonment in Scarborough Castle is typical of many:

> I was forced to lay out a matter of fifty shillings to stop out the rain and keep the room from smoking so much. When I had been at that charge, and made the room somewhat tolerable, they removed me into a worse room, where I had neither chimney nor fire-hearth. This being to the sea-side and lying much open, the wind drove in the rain forcibly, so that the water came over my bed, and ran about the room, that I was fain to skim it up with a platter. And when my clothes were wet, I had no fire to dry them; so that my body was numbed with cold, and my fingers swelled, that one was grown as big as two ... I was forced ... to hire one ... to bring me necessaries. Sometimes the soldiers would take it from her, and she would fight with them for it.°

Fox survived the temptation to bitterness, and when they sent 'a great company of Papists' to visit him, who affirmed the infallibility of the Pope, Fox argued with them with as much forthrightness and sincerity as ever he could have done had he been free:

> I told them if they were in the infallible spirit, they need not have jails, swords and staves, racks and tortures, fires and faggots, whips and gallows, to hold up their religion, and to destroy men's lives about it; for if they were in the infallible spirit they would preserve men's lives, and use none but spiritual weapons about religion.

As time went on, the winds sometimes blew less harshly, sometimes more, but whenever there was a heightened anxiety for the security of the throne, Quakers were among the bitterest sufferers. A declaration was made to try to convince the authorities that their fears were groundless, denying that Quakers ever had or ever would engage in treasonable practices.

> All bloody principles and practices we as to our own particular do utterly deny, with all outward wars and strife and fightings with outward

°*Journal.*

weapons for any end or under any pretence whatsoever... The Spirit
of Christ by which we are guided is not changeable, so as once to
command us from a thing as evil and again to move unto it; and we
do certainly know and so testify to the world that the Spirit of Christ,
which leads us unto all truth, will never move us to fight and war
against any man with outward weapons, neither for the kingdom of
Christ nor for the kingdoms of this world.°

But it was of no avail, and Friends continued to have their goods
confiscated and to languish in prison. This was usually achieved
by issuing a writ of *præmunire*, which had been used last to
punish Roman Catholic recusants in the days of Elizabeth, who
refused to take the oath of allegiance to the crown. The application of this method to Quakers implied that their refusal of the
oath of allegiance was of the same significance as the Popish
refusal, and thus blurred the enormous difference between a
political decision and an assertion that truth was too great a thing
for oaths.

During the first decade of the reign of Charles II a deliberate
attempt was made to exterminate the most undesirable non-
conformist elements in the country, and there was passed the
Second Conventicle Act, which made penalties easier to apply,
and offered to any who informed against the dissenters a reward
of a third of their goods. This provided a number of rogues with
a profitable occupation, so that one such informer, a certain inn-
keeper named William Thornaby, noted in his diary that he and
his agents had collected two thousand pounds in this way from
attacks on seventy-nine meetings. And while the persecution was
thus wide in scope it was also persistent and sustained in its
concentration on certain individuals. Isaac Penington, for example,
was imprisoned six times, including two years in a damp cell in
Aylesbury gaol, and nearly as long in Reading Gaol under
sentence of *præmunire*, and deprived of his estates. And William
Dewsbury was imprisoned in Warwick for periods lasting for
nineteen years, becoming too enfeebled to be able to walk any
distance when he was released, and finally dying of prison fever.

These men and women sustained a spirit of loving and
triumphant patience that kept the Society alive and its witness
pure. There were some who failed, but the corporate testimony
remained untouched by bitterness. There was Dewsbury himself,
writing from his last imprisonment to urge other Friends to be

°See Braithwaite, *The Second Period of Quakerism.*

ready to give up everything, wife and children and property and comfort,

> to give up our lives daily in tumults, strifes, bloodshed, with cruel sufferings, both in prison and when at liberty, for to bring enemies out of enmity in the light to be in union with God.°

Or there was Mary Dyer, executed for preaching in defiance of a sentence of banishment, of whom we are told

> then Mary Dyer was brought forth, and with a band of soldiers led through the town, the drums being beaten before and behind her, and so continued that none might hear her speak all the way to the place of execution, which was about a mile. Thus guarded, she came to the gallows, and being gone up the ladder, some said to her, that, if she would return home she might come down and save her life. To which she replied, 'Nay, I cannot, for in obedience to the will of the Lord I came, and in his will I abide faithful to death.°°

The most moving and significant of all these stories is the episode of James Nayler, illustrating as it does both the peculiar danger and the overwhelming triumph of the Quaker experience. He was a northerner, who joined the new movement in its earliest days, and came south to aid the work in London. There he fell in with flatterers, and became convinced that he was a special forerunner of the second coming of Christ, and he rode into Bristol on horseback, with his followers spreading clothes before him and singing, 'Holy, holy, holy, Lord God of Israel'. The authorities seized him and passed this savage sentence upon him:

> Resolved that James Nayler be set on a pillory, with his head in the pillory, in the New Palace, Westminster, during the space of two hours, on Thursday next, and be whipped by the hangman through the streets of Westminster to the Old Exchange, London, and there likewise, to be set upon the pillory, with his head in the pillory, for the space of two hours, between the hours of eleven and one, on Saturday next; in each of said places, wearing a paper containing an inscription of his crimes; and that at the Old Exchange, his tongue shall be bored through with a hot iron, and that he be there also stigmatized in the forehead with the letter B; and that he be, afterwards, sent to Bristol and be conveyed into and through the said city, on a horse bare ridged, with his face back, and there also publicly whipped the next market day after he comes thither; and that from thence he be committed to prison in Bridewell, London, and there restrained from the society of all people, and kept to

°*The Faithful Testimony ... of William Dewsbury.*
°°Besse: *A collection of the Sufferings of the People called Quakers from 1650-1689.*

hard labour till he be released by the Parliament; and, during that time, be debarred of the use of pen, ink, and paper, and have no relief but what he earns by his daily labour.

Nayler's response to the sentence was, 'God has given me a body; God will, I hope, give me a spirit to endure it. The Lord lay not these things to your charge.' The torture took its course, and during his imprisonment Nayler came to see and acknowledge his fault. He confessed it to Parliament, and succeeded in becoming reconciled to the Quaker leaders whom, by his folly, he had placed in increased jeopardy. To this point the story is a warning of the danger of the doctrine of the inward, personal dependence on the living Christ: this blasphemy, it might be argued, was the logical outcome of claiming to know Christ at first hand. If this argument were valid, there would have been others, particularly in such an age of religious excitement and lack of balance. But it did not in fact happen in any other case; and Nayler himself redeemed his error, not only by the loving patience of his endurance, but by the sublimity of his last words. If his error is a warning to humble Friends in their reliance on the Light within, these words uttered just before his death, are the highest expression of the Quaker attitude to persecution:

> There is a spirit which I feel that delights to do no evil, nor to revenge any wrong, but delights to endure all things, in hope to enjoy its own in the end. Its hope is to outlive all wrath and contention, and to weary out all exaltation and cruelty, or whatever is of a nature contrary to itself. It sees to the end of all temptations. As it bears no evil in itself, so it conceives none in thoughts to any other. If it be betrayed, it bears it, for its ground and spring is the mercies and forgiveness of God. Its crown is meekness, its life is everlasting love unfeigned; it takes its kingdom with entreaty and not with contention, and keeps it by lowliness of mind. In God alone it can rejoice, though none else regard it, or can own its life. It's conceived in sorrow, and brought forth without any to pity it, nor doth it murmur at grief and oppression. It never rejoiceth but through sufferings; for with the world's joy it is murdered. I found it alone, being forsaken. I have fellowship therein with them who lived in dens and desolate places in the earth, who through death obtained this resurrection and eternal holy life.

In the course of time toleration was discovered to be not so dangerous a course as men had supposed, and as the throne became secure dissent received permission to exist. When it did, Quakerism emerged strengthened by the persecution, strengthened in the ordinary, prudential sense by the purging it had gone through of unworthy elements; strengthened in a less prudential

sense by the triumphant love and patience represented by countless men and women utterly faithful in the extremity of trial.

This faithfulness, more than anything else, lent justification to
the otherwise arrogant claim that Quakerism represented a revival
of early Christianity. There were, as we have seen, significant
parallels: the emphasis on first-hand experience, the challenge to
tradition to re-examine its own foundations, the belief that God
still dealt in living communication with his people. But the early
Friends most closely followed their Master when they shared his
sufferings, not merely passively, suffering as one must under the
heel of tyranny, but actively, reaching out in love and tenderness
towards those who tortured them. Modern Friends find themselves
drawn to the study of these early days in the same kind of awe
and gratitude as they feel for the story of the early church. There
is no figure comparable to Christ: but there are men and women
comparable to the disciples, and the same atmosphere of explosive
love pervades them both. And when a modern Friend is acknow-
ledging his inadequacy to the demands of this generation, as like
as not he will compare himself and his contemporaries unfavour-
ably with the founders of the movement, not so much man by
man as a whole generation compared with another. And he
hankers after a new revival of fervour which should represent
'primitive Quakerism revived'.

That is perhaps the way they chiefly take their history, as a
source of challenge and inspiration: but it is necessary to tell the
story again because Quakerism cannot be understood without it.
When the spirit of God breaks into human life, the result is
activity directed to the needs of the age: the eternal love has a
contemporary form. Had the dynamic period of Quakerism come
at a different time, the whole history of the Society, and the form
of its modern preoccupations, would have been different.

Some of the seventeenth century flavour of Quaker thought was
merely idiosyncrasy. The connexion between honesty of purpose
and bluntness of manner, for example was characteristic of a time
of elaborate insincerity. A modern Friend can raise his hat to a
lady without feeling that he offers her more reverence than she
deserves, or that he is performing a merely meaningless gesture,
but the stand taken by early Friends in this matter is justified by
the stand the magistrates took in insisting on the honour. If they
set so much store by it, Friends were right to empty it of meaning.

Other oddities were not, even at the time, so essential, and

developed less happily. 'Theeing and thouing' was to the early
Friend an integral part of a whole testimony to the equality of
all men before the sight of God; but in the course of time it
developed into a form of intimate address, for Friends only, and
thus became an unintentional symbol of precisely the reverse.
Austere garments, too, were justified as a positive witness in a
time when the cost of clothes and the attention paid to them were
totally out of proportion. Pepys, for example, could write:

> Thence to the office, where busy till night, and then to prepare my
> monthly account, about which I staid till 10 or 11 o'clock at night, and
> to my great sorrow find myself £43 worse than I was the last month.
> But it hath chiefly arisen from my layings-out in clothes for myself and
> wife; viz., for her about £12, and for myself £55 or thereabouts;
> having made myself a velvet cloake, two new cloth suits, black, plain
> both, a new shagg gowne, trimmed with gold buttons and twist, with
> a new hat, and silk tops for my legs and many other things . . . . °

In answer to this, early Friends dressed in sombre clothes
which rapidly became a uniform; and despite the attempts of
liberal spirits to keep a reasonable freedom, the regulation costume
was as tyrannical as a monastic habit. Even so, it soon lost its
only justification, for it no longer carried its message of simplicity.
John Wesley, writing in 1746, complained that the traditional
garb was now more luxurious than that of other men:

> You retain just so much of your ancient practice, as leaves your present
> without any excuse . . . . What multitudes of you are very jealous as to
> the colour and form of your apparel—while in the most important, the
> expense, they are without any concern at all. They will not put on a
> scarlet or crimson stuff, but the richest velvet, so it be black or grave.
> They will not touch a coloured riband, but will cover themselves with a
> stiff silk from head to foot. They cannot bear purple; but make no
> scruple at all of being clothed in fine linen; yea to such a degree, that
> the linen of the Quakers is grown almost to a proverb.

In due time, this custom, too, withered away. The disappearance
of it is worth a little attention, for it illustrates at once the
dilemma and opportunity of modern Quakerism. In the first
instance, it will be remembered, Quaker grey was a witness to
the simplicity of soul and disregard of outward things which the
faithfulness to inward values demanded. Then it became a
tradition, not entirely without significance, but followed as part
of a withdrawal from the world. Then the rest of the world began
to dress more simply, until Quaker dress was distinct merely in

° *Diary.*

cut and uniformity; and thus it became a badge of peculiarity rather than a means of witness. Then, inevitably, it had to disappear, leaving the witness to simplicity without its traditional means of expression. It was the same with many of the other testimonies: the non-Quaker found his own method of expressing his democratic attitude by using the polite form 'you' for everyone instead of the familiar 'thou', and in other ways common sense has followed after Quaker insight, and left the Quakers with a tradition that had largely lost its meaning.

This raises the question, Has Quakerism any place in the modern world? Can a peculiar people, still with the marks of their seventeenth century origin upon them, bring their insight to bear upon the problems of a twentieth century world? The principle they have sought to express is clearly relevant and necessary. No one would deny that obedience to the law of God would bring man steadily closer to the fulfilment of his highest destiny. But it must be obedience to the law of God for this day, and not the law for a day that is gone. Can this be known?

It is to this question that the remainder of my argument is addressed. Quakerism has reached a point where it has almost completely shed the mere externals of its original witness. In the process, it has lost some of its vitality. But it contains, as the ground in early spring contains, unnoticed from without, the seeds of new life. Some of the 'oddities' of the seventeenth century testimony were related to perennial problems in human affairs; some to externals which then loomed large but have since disappeared. A modern expression of Quaker experience would give due emphasis to the eternal problems, and would also take account of modern difficulties which present themselves as peculiarly vicious to this generation. It is to this that we must now turn.

CHAPTER SIX

Living in the Light

THE central emphasis in the Quaker message has always been on the authority of the light within. It is from this that all the other peculiarities spring; and it is this which constitutes the excuse for the continued existence of a Quaker community.

In the early days, the authority of the spirit was seen largely in contrast with the authority of the Bible, because the alternative rival authority – that of the priesthood – had already been sufficiently challenged. When Milton wrote, 'New presbyter is old priest writ large', he was relying on a general consensus of opinion that priests were not to be uncritically obeyed. The Quaker definition of the doctrine of the inner light was thus conducted in opposition to the doctrine of an infallible Bible. If the Restoration had meant a return to Catholicism, Friends would have debated the merits of clerical authority more than they did. As it was, they were faced by an appeal to the text of scripture, and their main argument was thus directed to the need for a living interpretation rather than a literal obedience. They were thus among the first Christians to attack the fundamentalist position, and the argument advanced in the seventeenth century had an urgent relevance during the nineteenth, when the fundamentalist obstinacy was being beaten down by the sheer weight of scientific fact. Barclay's statement on the matter would serve for either period:

> Nevertheless, because they (the scriptures) are only a declaration of the fountain and not the fountain itself, therefore they are not to be esteemed the principal ground of all truth and knowledge, nor yet the adequate, primary rule of faith and manners, Yet, because they give a true and faithful testimony of the first foundation, they are and may be esteemed a secondary rule, subordinate to the Spirit, from which they have all their excellency and certainty: for, as by the inward testimony of the Spirit we do alone truly know them, so they testify that the Spirit is that Guide by which the saints are led into all truth: therefore, according to the Scriptures the Spirit is the first and principal Leader.[*]

[*] *Apology*.

The Quaker position was not that the Bible is full of errors, and therefore worthless; but that the spiritual guidance which set men writing the Bible is still available, both to convince us of the truth the Bible contains, and to correct any error that might have crept in. The 'Word of God', they argued, was the living Christ, spoken from all time to all time by the eternal God:

> In the beginning was the Word, and the Word was with God, and the Word was God. The same was in the beginning with God. All things were made by him; and without him was not anything made that was made. In him was life; and the life was the light of men ... And the Word was made flesh, and dwelt among us ... [*]

What men were to listen to was this Word, wherever they might hear him, in scripture, the voice of saintly men, and above all in the silence of their own hearts:

> The Canon of Scripture may be closed, but the inspiration of the Holy Spirit has not ceased. We believe that there is no literature in the world where the revelation of God is given so fully as in our New Testament Scriptures; we go back to them for light and life and truth. But we feel that the life comes to us, not from the record itself, but from communion with him of whom the record tells. Through his own Spirit we commune with him himself. In the words of Coleridge:—'I meet that in Scripture which finds me'. [**]

Looked at in one way, this seems a way of thinking that merely turns back upon itself: 'The Bible is true because it appeals to me as true.' This seems to leave open the whole issue, and to leave the way open for the indulgence of any whim or fancy that might exercise a momentary attraction. But it has never been so with Friends; and they were, indeed, pleading for a more responsible, not a less responsible, approach to the problems of belief and conduct.

When they rejected external authority, they were convinced that they were placing squarely upon the individual the responsibility for his own life to an extent that was impossible under authoritarian rule. For one thing, they argued, no external authority was even adequate: it could not prepare a man to meet all the difficulties of life, nor make his decisions for him in the trivial turns and twists of commonplace experience. No man can go through the day with a book of rules, or the memory of a set of sermons, or the injunctions of the confessional, and find in them

[*] *John*, 1, 1-4, 14.
[**] *Yearly Meeting Proceedings*, 1919.

guidance for all his perplexities. And though this is not, in fact, the way that a religious authority works, there is some ground for the argument that dependence on authority tends towards legalism, literalism in the following of rules. It was the danger which Jesus saw in the Jewish practice, and it is a danger which besets any religious regulation. What is mentioned in the rules may be faithfully followed, but the rest becomes of no great importance.

But this is surely fundamental to Christianity, the assertion that outward obedience to law of any sort is irrelevant beside the inward integrity, the insight, the dedication of heart, which springs from the love of God.

> Ye have heard that it was said by them of old time, Thou shalt not kill . . . . But I say unto you, That whosoever is angry with his brother without a cause shall be in danger of the judgement . . . .
> Ye have heard that it was said by them of old time, Thou shalt not commit adultery; But I say unto you, That whosoever looketh on a woman to lust after her hath committed adultery with her already in his heart . . . .°

No law, no authority can command the purposes of the heart, and if they are to be subdued to the will of God, they must be subdued by a power that grapples with them where they are.

If religion is to be progressive, developing, facing a new intellectual or cultural or moral situation fairly, and with genuine awareness of the real facts of the case, it must trust, in the end, to this principle, encouraging each generation to face its own problems – in the light of what it has learnt from the past, it is true – but in its own right, at the last, to make its own judgement on the present. And as this is true of a generation it is also true of each individual, who always faces, in the solitary, unique situation of his own life, a new, untried moral problem which he alone can deal with, for he alone can understand it. Continually do we find ourselves baffled in the attempt to give 'advice' to another about a personal decision, even such a relatively clear-cut issue as a change of occupation or the selling of a house. Much more does it defeat the power of one man to aid another in the intricacies of his spiritual and moral endeavour, in his relationship with his wife and children, his dealings with his fellow workers, and in the unfathomable depths of his growing sense of values.

If we claim, then, the right of the individual to think and judge

°*Matthew*, Ch. 5.

for himself, are we not simply demanding that the door be thrown open to anarchy? Is the Inner Light more than a splendid deception, a grand name for fantasy and self-will? Can man be left free to work out his own creed? Or must he have one forced upon him, at the point of a gun if he is old and incorrigible, in the classroom if there is still time to teach him? If he is to be left free, what is the authority that guides him?

For a time it was thought to be Reason, elevated for the moment to the semi-divinity of a capital letter. But the French Revolution, the triumph of Reason, soon tumbled the divinity off its throne, and for a generation the western world hurried back to the protection of authority. Then it was Liberalism, and man was freed again, except for some dragging economic chains. But even this was doomed, and two world wars have robbed humanity of its trust in humanity. Now the psychiatrists have added their ironic comment on the death of Reason, showing how our so-called logic follows the pattern of our unconscious desire, and how the reason of the most rational of us is at the mercy of distortions and deceptions that arise unbidden from an underground personality over which he has no control.

Reason is not enough. It is literally not enough, for it is but a part, a function of our personality subordinate to the whole. Like the digestive system, it has its own laws and its own rights, but by itself it is nothing. It has no power of its own to tame the beast it seeks to ride, and it can work by the laws of logic, without a flaw, and yet be tainted at the source. Nor does it reach far enough to touch the ultimate things of man's life. Philosophy can clear the issues and survey the ground, but the problems it leaves unsolved are the great ones. How shall a man find happiness, by seeking his own or seeking another's good? Where lies beauty, in the golden robe and jewelled crown, or in the dewdrop in a morning field? How shall a man save his soul alive? These questions could endure their tomes, and be no nearer their answer. And yet, and this is the urgency of the matter, they are questions to which each man finds his own answer in life, whether he knows it or not. No man can go to the end without having committed himself on these issues, and have sought his own happiness or another's, have lived simply or ostentatiously, and have lived either to life or death.

It is here that Quakers have claimed that man is not left alone. The alternative to an external authority is not whimsy or irrespon-

sible choice: it is a heightened responsibility in the belief that in
these matters, if we are faithful, we have the assurance of help
from the living spirit of God. The experience which has given rise
to this belief goes far too deep for words, and Friends have fallen
back perpetually on metaphor: the Light, the Seed, the Life.
Each metaphor contains its own message. It is the Light, for what
was puzzling to the reason becomes clear, as the problems of
mathematics become clear with the aid of a teacher. The Seed,
because when a man turns to this insight and follows it, it seems
to grow, to become stronger and more sure of its roots. And the
Life, because there is a sense of growing in it, of drawing from a
friendly source power to deal with the flaws in our personality
that had helped to darken our vision.

This is not, in normal Quaker experience, of the same
order as the ecstatic visions of mysticism. Occasionally, as we
should expect in such a tradition, there have occurred to Friends
overwhelming moments of insight, but they are not the grounds
of the doctrine of the Inner Light. This springs rather from a
quiet sense of being helped, of being personally sustained, and of
finding the complexities, which offered an impassable barrier to
the mind and will, suddenly, as if moved by an unseen hand, put
on one side so that the way is open that was before closed (and
indeed this word 'open', and 'openings', appears often among
Quaker metaphors).

This sense of divine accompaniment could be 'explained away'
in psychological terms, if it were not for one unfailing element. It
is not uncommon to be faced by doubts about a course of action,
or the assumption of an attitude; to struggle, and fail, to find a
solution; and then to wake up one morning with the whole way
clear before one – and the mechanism of this process could be
described in strictly materialistic terms. But no such explanation
will convince the Quaker that his clarification is a mere settling
of his own account with himself, for there is a consistent *kind of
solution* which he perpetually meets. When, over and over again,
he is beckoned along a path that goes counter to his own interests,
and comes, the further he goes along it, to resemble more and
more the road to Calvary, then it is impossible to dismiss the
haunting certainty that these openings are the work of the living
Christ.

Friends have always been much exercised over the relationship
between the Inward Light and the Risen Christ, both in the early

days when they were anxious to establish the extent of their own orthodoxy against the misrepresentation of their enemies, and later, when other, more theologically minded denominations began to ask awkward questions. No theologically satisfactory answer has been produced*; but nothing can shake the Quaker belief that when he puts at the service of his Master all the thought and study and resolve he is capable of, and brings his perplexity to the Light, he will see something more in consequence, something he had not been able to find by his own efforts; and that something more will seem to be contributed by the loving hand of Christ. To this principle he believes he must trust himself, believing that despite its risks, it offers a hope of fuller, richer, more obedient life. The safest way to avoid error is to be dead: the way of the greatest danger offers the hope of the most triumphant service.

This belief does not preclude, as I have said, the possibility of error; but there have always been present in Quaker thinking certain safeguards, which offer some protection without suppressing the life.

The first of these lies in the whole character of the movement and the circumstances of its origin. The doctrine of the Inner Light is the religious equivalent of the claim of the scientist to the right to see for himself; and the Quaker expression of the doctrine has always included a measure of scientific matter-of-factness. The Inner Light is not a substitute for the facts of the situation: it is an aid to the interpretation and evaluation of the facts. And for this reason Quakers have traditionally studied science, and achieved distinction in it out of all proportion to their numbers.** When it is thus subdued to plain facts and rooted in the empirical the individual judgement is safe from a vast field of error, safer, indeed, than a religious or doctrinal authority, which can deny the facts of science as long as it has power to suppress the scientist. The same principle preserves the rights of reason to the very limit of its authority, and ensures that individual judgement operates at its proper level. When a man thinks straight, he thinks with God, and there can be no conflict

*Though see Edward Grubb: *The Historic and the Inward Christ*, Swarthmore Lecture 1914.

**See Ruth Fry: *Quaker Ways*, and her estimate that 'judging by the statistics between 1851 and 1900 a Quaker or man of Quaker descent had forty-six times more chance of election as a Fellow of the Royal Society than his fellow countrymen'.

between the Light and the work of reason within its own sphere.

In consequence of this, the Society of Friends has always paid great attention to education, and to education of a particular sort. The possibility of the guidance of God is no justification for neglecting the mental capacities we already possess; and from the first Quakers have been busy with schools and multitudinous informal methods of education of young and old.

The other safeguard, developed to a unique extent in the Society of Friends, is an organization that permits the enlightenment of one judgement by another, without setting one above the other; and provides for the exercise together of the waiting and seeking that permits the truth to be found. To this problem, too, Fox turned his attention, and the latter half of his public life was concerned with organization to a degree he could not have expected when he first set out with his message.

These are the two main lines of defence against the dangers of individual error. Men can be misled by their own desires, or deceived by the errors of others, and can claim for their illusion the sanctity of a divine command. And because of this it is necessary to protect them in two ways: first by reducing as far as possible their vast capacity for error by the training of the intellect and the development of a harmonious personality; and second, by the setting of one judgement against another, so that in any conflict the two views may be set side by side and judged by the fact of the historic Christ. These safeguards do not eliminate risk altogether; and if they did, they would remove Quakerism from the true line of Christian development, from the whole hazardous experiment to which God entrusted his world when he set man free to choose right or wrong, life or death, heaven or hell. The belief in the Inner Light is a belief that in thus laying the creation open to man's futility, God knew what he was about, and in giving man the capacity to go wrong, he gave him also the capacity to see and respond to the divine purpose, knowing that in the fullness of time man would see the light.

And the life was the light of men. And the light shineth in darkness, and the darkness comprehended it not.

CHAPTER SEVEN

Education

THE Quaker attitude to education is important not only for its judgement on the problems of education itself, but for the way it illustrates the doctrine of the Inner Light from which it springs. Friends have always, from the days of Fox's most active ministry, set great store by education, and by a particular form of it. They parted company, both in theory and practice, with the educational principles of their day, for they were based on a doctrine of man wholly unacceptable to Quaker experience. Man, the old theory would run, was born evil, and depended on education to be made good. His natural impulses were of the devil, and the parent and schoolmaster were compelled to curb them and eradicate them by whatever means seemed necessary. In the service of this compulsive discipline, there was a curriculum of classical language and biblical and theological study which drew its strength from its very difficulty.

In contrast to this, there arose in the seventeenth century a liberal view of both the curriculum and the methods of discipline based on a more humane doctrine of man. Natural impulse was welcomed and trained, rather than suspected and repressed, and curiosity about the world, and a certain childish irresponsibility of behaviour, were seen to be harmless in themselves and perhaps even valuable in the process of growth. This latter liberal humanism was to find relatively little expression in practice for two hundred years, after Rousseau and his followers, Spencer and other scientific thinkers, and the modern school of psychologists had all worked their slow effect on the life of school and home.

In the days of the early Friends, the conflict between the old view and the new was still very unequal. The old view was entrenched in habit, which is of as much influence in educational affairs as in any – and perhaps more than most. Furthermore, the theoretical conflict was prejudiced because it appeared to be a conflict between a religious and an irreligious view of man. The old belief was tied up with the fundamentals of Christian doctrine, the original sinfulness of humanity, the work of redemption in the sacrifice of Jesus on the Cross, and the work of divine grace in the continued redemption of the church through confession and absolution and sacrament. And the reformed church, though it might alter the means of grace, setting less store by the work of the priesthood, still took the same view of fallen man, now intensified indeed, and calling for sterner measures to eradicate the sinful impulses to joy and frivolity. The Puritan regarded human nature as more corrupt that the medieval church had ever done, and natural activities were banned ever more vigorously as dissent found itself more on the defensive. In such a context, the arguments of the humanists seemed merely anti-christian. To argue that natural curiosity and spontaneous impulse were of positive value to the growing child was not merely to deny a fundamental doctrine, but to threaten a whole self-consistent theological and practical system. Like the Copernican attack on the medieval cosmogony, it seemed to threaten far more than the point of attack. Not only would the church itself be beaten back from the educational field, but a new generation of men would grow up, without religion, without grace, living by animal impulse. Even the Quaker was nervous about *this* possibility:

All natural tongues and languages upon the earth make no more than natural men; and the natural man knows not the things of God.°

In its simplest terms, and to borrow the metaphor which was to become the battle-cry of Rousseau and Froebel, the choice was between two views of education: first, as a process of stamping or moulding, the making of a coin; and second, as a process of growth, like the development of a plant. On the first view, the task of parent and schoolmaster was to force the right 'shape' on the plastic material of childhood. On the second, the teacher has merely to devise the right conditions of healthy growth, and the child will do the rest, under the law of his own nature.

The Quaker belief about the nature of man was different from both of these, and produced a unique theory of education. Man is not in himself good or bad, but his qualities and faculties can be illuminated by the light of God shining directly on them and through them. This is the most significant thing about man, this capacity for the ultimate freedom of the spirit to know God at first hand. The rigours of the disciplinary view were thus rejected,

°Fox: *Gospel Truth Demonstrated.*

because they did harm to the life of God in the individual; while the greater liberty of the other view could be accepted without at the same time implying that man can simply do as he pleases.

But is not this merely a pious way of saying the same thing as the libertarians – leaving man free to follow his impulse while pretending that he was finding God? Is this not to equate the inner light with individual whim? And so we find ourselves back at the fundamental problem. The answer is to be found in the actual content of Quaker education, which has never given support for this extreme individualist and naturalist theory. What, the Quaker theory would run, is the nature of the 'ultimate freedom of the spirit' to which our education is to tend? The word freedom means nothing unless it is qualified: it is not a noun, so to speak, but a transitive verb; and nobody is ever free, simply and absolutely. There are, it would seem, two elements present in the liberty we are discussing: first, the freedom to grasp at truth for oneself, to make one's own contact with reality, which I will call freedom of insight; and secondly the freedom of moral choice which at its highest is the freedom to love God. Insight and love, then, are the two aspects of the freedom of the spirit. And except in the service of this kind of freedom, mere freedom of action – the third part of the trilogy of knowledge, feeling and will – is of no particular importance. There must be some limitations on freedom of action; and the nature of the limitations will be determined by the purpose for which the freedom is needed.

To discover the limitations on freedom of action, then, we must first discover the limitations on freedom of insight and love. What are the limits of a child's ability to see truth for himself? And what are the limits on his power to love, to respond to truth in personal commitment?

There are two important limits on the power of insight: ignorance and prejudice: first, ignorance, because until certain facts have been brought to our attention, we cannot see for ourselves. If we walk through the countryside ignorant of botany and ornithology and geology, the walk may be enjoyable, but it is a green confusion compared with the same walk when we have learnt from the scientist how to use our eyes. There are few flowers to be seen until we have learnt to look, and we cannot have insight without the facts. And for these facts, we need the help of other men's observation, accepting it not in place of our own but as the ground and stimulus of our own. The same is true of the ultimate freedom of spiritual insight: in the end man is free, and able, to grasp at truth for himself, but he must first have the aid of other observation and discovery. Insight is prevented by ignorance.

It is also hampered by prejudice, which I use loosely to cover the whole tendency of the mind to close upon an issue before it is in possession of all the facts. We 'inherit' some prejudices from our parents, copying or revolting against their opinions according to our nature. We jump to conclusions. We accept a welcome half-truth without proceeding to test it and explore it to the end; or reject an unwelcome half-truth without looking for the part that concerns us. All this, the kind of faulty mental equipment which might be described as the original sin of the intellectual life, all militates against the power of insight.

If these are the two chief barriers to insight, love has its own versions of the same difficulties. The chief here is self-love, the tendency to regard ourselves as not only the centre but the circumference and area of our own universe. This self interest is the equivalent to love of ignorance to understanding. It is the darkness of the heart; and we cannot begin to love until the darkness begins to dissipate. We cannot even love man if we are wrapped up in self; and we cannot love God until we have learnt to love his children:

> He that loveth not his brother whom he hath seen, how can he love God whom he hath not seen?°

The other obstacle, which is to love what prejudice is to understanding, is mental conflict, the divided self, the clash of ideal and lust, noble impulse and the powerful urge of base desire.

> For the good that I would I do not; but the evil that I would not, that I do.°°

And it is equally true that the good that I would *love*, I do not love enough, and I continue to love the evil that I am learning to hate. Our heart may fail our insight:

> I see, not feel, how beautiful they are,°°°

wrote Coleridge. And as prejudice, conditioning, and the rest, distort our vision of truth, so emotional disturbances prevent our

°*1 John*, 4, 20.
°°*Romans*, 7, 19.
°°°*Dejection*.

developing the right attitude. 'Lord that I might love thee,' ran an old prayer, 'as I might have loved thee had I not sinned against thee.'

Now to educate for the ultimate freedom of the Inner Light is to educate for this, that children should gain the knowledge they need to sustain judgement, should cure the prejudices acquired in the past – personal or racial – should begin to love men as the first turning of their interest away from themselves, and should be freed from the mental conflict which so paralyses emotion and action. In all these directions, there is a contribution which the educator, parent or teacher or friend, can make, indeed must make, without infringing on the ultimate prerogative of liberty. The ultimate goal of learning to swim is to be free of the sustaining hand in the water; yet the sustaining hand is a necessity in the learning process. And so with education for liberty of the spirit. A measure of educational control is the sustaining hand.

The first requirement is the imparting of knowledge. There can be no insight apart from knowledge, and the boy at school, in his preparation for freedom of understanding, must acquire certain knowledge by the direction of his teachers. We cannot control his vision when he reaches the top of the mountain, but we must control his efforts to get to the top. If, as occasionally happens, he sees a short cut for himself, or chooses one path from several that we lay before him, well and good. But it is our responsibility to ensure that the paths we open up do, in fact, lead to the top, and not down into a dark valley on the other side. This is our responsibility for the curriculum, and it includes the curriculum of religious knowledge. There is a fatal flaw in the argument that we must not 'teach' religion because that is indoctrination: we must leave the child free to choose for himself when he is grown up, but we cannot evade the responsibility of the choice of curriculum. If we choose not to teach something we forbid the child to learn it: if we do teach it, we do not forbid him to forget it. A boy can choose to remember or forget his Latin when he leaves school; but if he has learnt no Latin at school, he has no choice in the matter.

We must, then, select the curriculum. But if we are to educate for insight, we must select a curriculum on which insight can be used. And insight, in the wide sense I am using the word, involves some sort of ultimate value judgement, the possibility of a personal committal, a recognition of and response to something eternally worth while. This would point to a curriculum that can appeal directly to a child's sense of values, the curriculum, in the terms of educational theory, of 'interest', the knowledge which offers the boy an opportunity of being personally involved, of feeling that it matters to him now. (In practice it is necessary to qualify the word 'now' in the last sentence. It is clear that certain knowledge can be given to a boy because he will find it valuable later – learning his tables, a foreign language and such like – and anyone may be expected to spend some of his present time in the service of the future. But if all a boy's time is spent in this way, he cannot learn insight: as a man who saves all his income cannot keep alive. The problem is not one of principle but of proportion).

It was precisely this curriculum of interest that the early Friends demanded for their children. George Fox advised the setting up of schools for instruction in 'whatsoever things were civil and useful in the creation.'* Penn wrote to his wife asking for a broad curriculum for their own children:

> Let it be useful knowledge, such as is consistent with Truth and godliness . . . the useful parts of mathematics, as building houses or ships, measuring, surveying, dialling, navigation . . . agriculture . . . let my children be husbandmen and housewives . . . This leads to consider the works of God and nature, of things that are good, and diverts the mind from being taken up with the vain arts and inventions of a luxurious world . . Be sure to observe their genius and do not cross it as to learning; let them not dwell too long on one thing, but let their change be agreeable, and all their diversions have some little bodily labour in them.**

And he writes in similar strain in *Some Fruits of Solitude*:

> We press their memory too soon, and puzzle, strain and load them with words and rules; to know Grammar and Rhetorick, and a strange Tongue or two, that it is ten to one may never be useful to them: Leaving their natural Genius to Mechanical and Physical, or natural Knowledge uncultivated and neglected . . . Children had rather be making of Tools and Instruments of Play; Shaping, Drawing, Framing and Building, etc., than getting some Rules of Propriety of Speech by Heart . . . It were Happy if we studied Nature more in natural Things; and acted according to Nature . . . Let us begin where she begins, go her pace, and close always where she ends, and we cannot miss of being good Naturalists.

Thus, in contrast with the narrow, classical curriculum of the time – and of the generations to follow – the early Friends launched

*Journal.
**Janney, *The Life of William Penn*.

upon a broad study of nature and man. Certain peculiar prejudices were to creep in, such as the violent refusal to permit music in Friends' schools, even to the extent of banning spontaneous singing while walking about the school; but in general Friends' schools remained faithful to their principle. In particular they were pioneers of scientific study, especially that kind of science which brings children into first-hand relationship with the world of nature, the living facts of the universe. Thus Bootham, the boys' school at York, was the first school in England to possess a Natural History Society, in 1834; and from the other schools come reports during the middle years of the nineteenth century (when the public schools were still confined to Latin, Greek, and a little mathematics) of collections of fossils, exhibitions of botanical collections, the development of astronomy. 'We try,' said a report on the work at Bootham in 1864, 'to cultivate everything for which any boy has a sort of taste.'[*]

Today the broad curriculum is accepted for all schools, but the Quaker schools preserve their characteristic emphasis in out-of-school activities, where a boy who has followed the generally accepted grammar-school curriculum in class may find two or three or more activities to suit his own bent, chosen from a wide range of possibilities: pottery, aero-modelling, leather-work, silver-beating, bookbinding, bird-ringing, and the whole range of normal boyish pastimes in the way of games and hobbies.

This, then, is the way Quaker education has sought to supply the first need of the mind reaching out to the light: the humble acceptance of mere fact, as wide and as systematic as could be grasped. The inward light cannot be all darkness if the first act of the growing mind was to fling open as many windows as possible onto the world.

The other obstacle to insight is prejudice. The answer to this lies not so much in curriculum as in method. We cure ourselves of prejudice when we acquire the capacity for and habit of self-criticism, independent judgement, and working things out for ourselves. This involves a teaching method based not on telling but on setting to find out, not on acceptance but on testing and demonstrating. For this reason, Quaker schools have made a variety of experiments in various heuristic methods of learning. At one time they were making considerable use of the Dalton plan. They have experimented with film-production, with discussion-group

° Newcastle Commission, vol. IX.

techniques, with local surveys, with a shop run as an economics project; and in the general course of routine work the library and individual investigation have for many years played a large part. At times the critical spirit thus engendered has been irresponsible; at times it has failed to appear; but the general trend of Quaker education is towards the production of a responsible open-mindedness.

Of the two obstacles to love, the first is the imprisonment of the self within its own concerns. Here the child needs help from outside before he can stir. He must be loved before he can love. The initial response goes back, as we have today come to see, to babyhood, but there is still an essential function here which the school must fulfil. There must be people for him to love, people who need him, and whose need of him he can recognize. These will not normally be the staff, but the boys and girls who make up the school community. For this reason Quaker schools have always been small, and until recently were self-consciously conducted along 'family' lines. As they have had to increase in size, from sheer economic necessity, they have sought the means of preserving the sense of responsible community which mere size might destroy. They have thus devised school councils, self-governing school societies, and free time for the spontaneous group-activities that boys will always engage in if the opportunity is there. This kind of group-life enables the boy, even the odd, incompetent boy who cannot play games or act on the stage, to find that he is wanted by other people, not for anything remarkable he can do, but because he is himself, and has individuality to contribute to the common life. So he may grow outwards and discover the sense of interrelatedness that lies dimly below the threshold of consciousness.

Finally, the growing child is held back from the freedom to love by his own emotional disorganization. He is Jekyll and Hyde, or a whole battlefield of Jekylls and Hydes. He cannot achieve loving insight until he has begun to be a whole person, with a unified pattern underlying his responses. The beginner at cricket is clumsy because he concentrates attention on one part of his body and the rest looks after itself. The skilled batsman is pleasant to watch because the whole of him responds to the situation, and foot and ankle are as much involved in meeting the threat of the ball as the eye and hand. We cannot love without some measure of self-control, as we cannot steer a ship on an errand of mercy until we can manage the rudder. And to this end, the boy needs help from an ordered discipline, in which he may learn self-control with the aid of a measure of control from without. Some part of him wishes to respond in a certain way, but is powerless to control the part that wishes otherwise; and he needs help in dealing with the rebellious part of himself.

This help comes in the shape of an established routine, a settled rhythm of things the boy has to do whether he likes them or not. The system will be wisely planned, and will respond to the boy's nature as the scaffolding responds to the plan for the building; but the scaffolding will be there as the building grows and will prevent it from shooting out a loggia or a gable or a bridge of sighs. The qualification here is that the design of the scaffolding should be generally acceptable to the boy. It may be a rigid one, and the discipline be severe, provided that it represents what the boy at his best will approve. Boys will accept the iron hand of the dramatic producer when they are keen to act; and they will similarly accept this framework of authority if they can perceive its justification in the total growth of their personality, and the necessities of corporate life. If it is not accepted, the discipline becomes the stamping, moulding external influence which must fail to assist the growth of the spirit.

Such a system is not easy to devise, and in recent years Friends' schools have all been experimenting with their discipline, ranging from the libertarianism of the years after the first world war to the more cautious, tighter hand of today. Whatever the degree of external control, there is always an effort to ensure that the boys or girls themselves take sufficient share in the planning to enable them to accept the final result. The 'final result' has always involved a certain measure of punishment, and there is no reason why it should not. Indeed, when the boys were asked to make their own suggestions for the revision of a punishment system in force at one of the schools just after the second war, they replied at once that they would consider the problem, but wished to say at the outset that they hoped that whatever revision would be decided upon, it would not result in merely reducing the weight of punishment available. Punishment, of a routine, impersonal variety, is but the slightly painful warning that something is wrong, as indigestion is a warning that all is not well with the nutritive system.

These are the principles of Quaker education: the wide, realist curriculum, a teaching method based on first-hand enquiry, a living, active school community with ample opportunity for individual responsibility, and a framework of acceptable routine.

There have from time to time been deviations from this tradition, as there have from many fundamentals of Quaker witness, but they can be seen clearly as deviations, and not the true current of thought. One such departure was the development of the idea of a 'guarded' education for Quaker children, a closed protective school and home life that should enable the child to find his feet, as it were, before exposing him to the winds of controversy or the opinions of secular men. This tendency is common enough in a religious sect that has lost the explosive conviction of its original inspiration and has found itself forced on the defensive. That phase has passed, and the genuine tradition remains. Friends' schools are now full of Quaker doings, but there are other things too: church attendance for the many boys and girls (over half the total) members of other denominations; the study of church history on a wider basis than Quaker history; co-operation with other schools; adventurous excursions in England and abroad; and a great variety of work with non-sectarian bodies – Youth Committees, Community centres, Scouts, work camps and the like. The religious policy of the schools is now more nearly that of the early Friends than ever it was: to start people questing for the truth wherever the search may lead, not defending a prepared position, but setting children scurrying across any country that might seem to offer the likelihood of discovery. And this not negatively, with indifference and the false 'neutrality' that is in fact denial of the importance of the search, but positively, with all the discovery and conviction the community can claim laid out to stimulate and guide the search.

Another apparent deviation, which still causes the Society some embarrassment, is the odd situation in which a democratic community finds itself possessed of a number of 'public' schools charging high fees, in a day when the public schools are attacked as undemocratic. The trouble here is that the Society has been caught by a turn in the climate of opinion which has distorted the original meaning of their efforts. Like all sections of the church, they felt the need for schools in which their own children could learn what they needed to learn of their own religious heritage, and they did no more than other Christians when they copied the existing schools in this way. In this there is nothing 'undemocratic', for there is no suggestion of exclusion: these were not schools which everyone wanted to attend, or from which all but a few were excluded.

When the state came into the field of educational provision, however, the public schools became the object of envious glances, because they seemed to represent a closed world within which was confined the competition for the privileged positions of society. The public schools, it was said, (and with justification) got most of the best 'jobs'. The Quaker boarding schools are not, most of them, public schools in the generally accepted meaning of the word, but they all come under this widespread condemnation of being within the charmed circle.

The problem is at once too complicated and ultimately too trivial to be debated here. The embarrassment is genuine, and Friends have frequently discussed it, but can see no way of making any radical change, apart from abandoning the essential purpose of the schools. And so for the present the matter stands there, until the state takes up the issue again or economic conditions compel a new approach, or someone can see a way out of the tangle. There can be no doubt, however, that the genuine Quaker motive is still that the work the Society is called upon to do demands some sort of special educational provision – not, be it noted, a 'better' provision than that open to the children of non-Quaker parents – that particular problem is being slowly and inevitably solved by the steady improvement in public education – but a different provision, in which boys and girls can be stirred with a greater hope and set looking for truth on a deeper level than they might elsewhere.

This, then, is the first safeguard against the errors of individualism, a view of education which ensures a welcome to all light, provides an opportunity for the growth of loving community, and calls for the dedication of the mind and will. These principles could be followed into the variety of Quaker activity in the field of adult education: their work in the adult school movement, and in educational settlements; the summer schools and conferences for members of the Society; the founding of Woodbrooke, a residential settlement for the study of the Christian faith and its implications in social and economic and political life; and all the varied means by which the education of a 'lay ministry' is achieved. But these introduce no distinctive principle: they merely develop to the full the principles we have already considered. These things are not done from a belief in the power of education to do everything. They rest rather on the belief that a full education is man's offering to God's purposes, and that His spirit will ripen the growing life to its fruit.

CHAPTER EIGHT

Insight and Love

THE rôle of education may be defined as the creation of the conditions of insight: bringing men into the state of readiness when they may be most sensitive to the light. But the insight itself, the final response to the light, remains beyond the control of any external conditions. It is an affair of the inmost life, beyond logic though not counter to it, beyond language beyond the normal rules of expectation. The process of education cannot, therefore, 'guarantee' that when a man comes to deal thus with fundamental reality he will be sure to come to a right decision. The problem of dealing with errant insight still remains, then, even when education has done its utmost. The individual must be free to come at truth for himself, or he can never reach it: but how can society – and even the individual himself – be protected against the possibility of error?

This is not, of course, an exclusively religious problem. It is the root difficulty of any theory of government except the most abstract and extreme authoritarianism and the most abstract anarchy – and neither of these abstractions has ever occurred in reality. In normal practice, there is an awkward border-line between freedom and regulation, which varies in different circumstances, but always represents a roughly understood convention of what a man may be expected to decide for himself and what he may expect to be told by those in authority. In the secular state planned to promote the greatest happiness of the greatest number, regimentation is at the minimum, and individuals are left free to determine the source of their own happiness within such limits as will prevent them interfering seriously with the happiness of their neighbours. There is thus a perpetual argument on points of detail, and the civil courts are full of neighbours seeking to prove that they have or have not interfered with each other's happiness; and the police courts are full of people who have offended against rules laid down to protect the comfort and well-being of the people at large. This is a universal problem, the point of contact between rights and duties, between individual well-being and public well-being.

But though this argument is common to secular and religious societies, it is the religious society that raises it to its most acute form. In the secular society, two individuals can find their happiness in entirely different ways without coming into conflict with each other. One can decide that cricket makes the highest contribution to human happiness, while the other awards the palm to golf; and though they differ thus fundamentally, they may live together in complete harmony within the one society: one can spend his time on the village green, the other on the links. This is possible because each is seeking only the happiness of himself. But as soon as a religious element enters the argument, the tension is raised at once. If the cricketer and the golfer now seek to establish that one pursuit is more pleasing than the other *to God*, the problem becomes much more urgent.

This particular conflict is, it is to be hoped, unlikely to occur, but it represents the fundamental difficulty that besets any attempt to base ethics on religious belief. If man has only himself to please, he may hope for a reasonable compromise or some means of letting different men go their own way. But if he has God to please, the way he acts is no longer a matter of indifference to all but himself. Nothing he does matters to himself alone. There is thus a temptation to interfere with the lives of other men, and to compel naughty and irreverent people to fall into line with a high moral ideal. A theocracy, in other words, has a temptation to become more authoritarian than a secular democracy, because its subjects are being kept in order, as it were, both for their good and for the greater glory of God. Social discipline is heightened by the tremendous stakes, which now become no less than eternal salvation; and the cosmic order seems involved in the most trivial ethical, or even ritual, matter.

The Quaker judgement on this issue removes this particular source of tension by claiming that the authority to interpret the will of God is available for all men. There can be no hierarchy of authority because any member of the community might find himself being used, as the prophets were used, to speak for God. The difficulty removed is, however, replaced by another: how to determine whether or not the prophet is speaking for God or for himself. We have seen how education may be used to ensure that before a man does so speak he will have been exposed to a religious tradition, considered it in a spirit of critical judgement and at the same time loving humility, and will have brought to the issue the considered response of whole, integrated personality. But still, when education has succeeded thus far – and it must be confessed that education is not certain to succeed thus far – still the issue is not safe. Obedience to the rules of hygiene does not ensure bodily health; and obedience to the 'rules' of insight does not mean that the individual is certain to be right. There must thus be always a measure of uncertainty as to how far an individual may be trusted, particularly when what he says is in any sort of conflict with tradition. There is no technique for the recognition of true prophecy.

The first question the Quaker would raise in his approach to this problem would be: Does the disagreement matter? Is the particular quarrel of any real importance? And in more general terms, is unity of belief essential to Christians? Or unity of action? Or any sort of unity?

It is clear that there must be some sort of unity at a fundamental level which members of the same religious group will accept, or there is no need for the group to exist at all. If religion is a response to ultimate reality, then members of a religious group must share some common element in their response. They must to some extent believe in the same sort of reality, and their beliefs will express themselves in some degree of common language and action. A religious anarchy in which every individual has his own private religion, utterly unrecognizable to anyone else, and postulating its own spiritual order, is the religion of insanity. There would be no argument between Quakers and other Christians on this point. There can be but one reality, however differently different people apprehend it; and a religious group derives its justification and gains its impetus from the extent to which its members find themselves talking the same spiritual language and expressing their insight in the same kind of conduct.

The argument would concern itself with the *level of apprehension* at which unity is essential. Religious awareness is the deepest human experience, and it is discovered below the surface of word and act, in the silent loneliness in which, in the end, each man lives. This discovery is something that no man can fully describe. He may begin to speak of it, haltingly, and act in the light of it, uncertainly; but the whole meaning of it, its glory, is not to be shared. Yet though it is so private, it is here that unity *matters*. People are drawn together into religious fellowship because they find, by odd echoes of speech or deed, that they have found in the depths of their own lives something of the same order as others have discovered in theirs. Christians usually describe this experience as the love of Christ, by which they mean that the personality of Jesus has touched them in the way that a human being whom they love and admire touches them; that they have found themselves trying to please him, to 'express' him in their own deeds; and that between the two poles, of deep, spontaneous love and worship, and the deliberate bending of the will in service, they begin to sense a living relationship in which it seems, tremendously, miraculously, that God himself is putting them in place in the life of his world.

This acceptance of the lordship of Christ and the strange sense of knowing him and being used by him is the characteristically Christian experience, and it represents, for each man, a response to the same reality. Christians can, as it were, recognize each other's experience by their own, as a mother knows what another mother feels. And when they come to describe their experience in language, despite the utter inadequacy of the medium of words, there is a certain resemblance between one description and another. When the description is pressed further into the intellectual interpretation of it, into the deductions which may be made about the nature of reality, there is still a measure of unity to be perceived. When experience is turned into theology, there emerges a consistent system of thought. This measure of intellectual unity is a very important element in the total Christian experience. If a number of men are taken separately into a private room, and there are shewn a picture, and then they are brought out and made to describe what they have seen; then when their descriptions tally in fundamentals though they differ in detail it may be assumed that they have indeed seen the same picture. It is thus with Christian experience and thought: the details differ, but the general outline of the picture is to be recognized in the varying accounts.

It is particularly important that Christian thought and action should be united at certain points of tension in the world's thought and action. If there is any truth in the private experience of reality, then the public expression of it will be united on the crucial intellectual and ethical issues of human life. While individual variation may be reasonable on a fine point of morals, there is a difference between what Paul calls 'the works of the flesh',*

> Adultery, fornication, uncleanness, lasciviousness, idolatry, witchcraft, hatred, variance, emulations, wrath, strife, seditions, heresies, envyings, murders, drunkenness, revellings

and such like, and the 'fruits of the spirit',

> love, joy, peace, longsuffering, gentleness, goodness, faith, meekness, temperance.

And as the inward experience makes some such broad, recognizable difference to a man's outward behaviour, so it must make some broad difference to his intellectual presentation of it. It is for this reason that the Christian church found itself compelled to design its creeds. These were statements carefully, if controversially, arrived at to indicate where Christians stood in relation to some broad division of human thought. Today they seem sometimes to be concerned with trifling issues, but they were not trifling in their day. The celebrated 'cleavage over a diphthong', the controversy at Nicea on whether Christ were to be regared as *homo-ousios,* of the same substance as the Father, or *homoi-ousios,* of like substance, has caused many men (including Carlyle) much mirth, but it represented in truth a vital principle. For at the time the world had not emerged entirely from the religious conception represented by the Greek pantheon, and men were ready to look on Christ as a sort of Apollo, living in a Jewish Olympus along with his father, Jupiter-Jehovah. The choice between the two words was thus a choice between two religions, two utterly different approaches to reality, with as wide an ethical cleavage as that between Paul's 'flesh' and 'spirit'.

The great creeds of the church are thus an attempt to indicate, by a sort of remote projection, the nature of the essential Christian experience. If in the privacy of their heart, the argument would run, men have had the same *kind* of experience of reality, then its sameness will appear in the intellectual and moral sphere along certain broad lines. But while this was correct, and historically necessary, it is incorrect to argue, as church authorities went on to argue, that the unity of the church is to be ensured by adherence to a creed. Describe your experience, and compare your descriptions, by all means; and if the descriptions

*Galatians, 5, 19.

are the same, then the experience was probably the same too. But to set up a standard description does not guarantee that men will achieve a standard experience. A hundred men can recite the same creed and yet have a hundred different religions — or none. And in times of acute religious conflict it is beside the point to set up rival creeds as battle-standards, under which the parties may enrol themselves.

It is beside the point, for the simple reason that most of the party will not understand the issue. Creeds that spring from first-hand inward experience have their clear value as an attempt to describe the experience, and provide a suggestive standard whereby the individual may assess his own. But creeds set up as slogans are taken hold of intellectually by those who have not reached them from the depths of their own life. In the seventeenth century this is precisely what was happening. Credal statements, liturgical practice, moral codes had the effect of dividing one group from another. They were the badges of the armies. But they were, in the main, badges which the rank and file took on trust from their generals, and did not find in the reality of their own life.

It was this that prompted the Quaker rejection of creeds. All that mattered, they claimed, was the inward experience; and the form of words was irrelevant and mischievous. Not only were they barriers between men: they were barriers between a man and his own soul, for as soon as someone was committed in public to a certain religious doctrine, he was almost prevented from following honestly the leading of the light within. The only possible position was to permit complete freedom of religious belief, and not to be shocked, as it were, or persecute for any cause whatsoever. Only thus could men be rallied to the necessity for seeking the truth within. Creeds might be regarded as crutches, with which a man could obtain the effect of walking without using his legs. But men were made to walk: let them fling away their crutches, and then it would be seen who *could* walk; and all men would soon walk for themselves.

Naturally such a revolutionary attitude caused hostility out of all proportion to the cause: it is the way of humanity to be suspicious of men who throw aside the rules and regulations of conventional life. And as the early Christians were suspected of blasphemous views and dark, unimaginable vice, so the Quakers were suspected of anarchy, blasphemy and immorality. They took

considerable pains, indeed, to defend themselves, and much of
the Quaker apologetic of the time is more orthodox in form than
it would have been if the writers had not been so anxious to
defend themselves against the charge of unorthodoxy. Wishing
to prove themselves Christians, they made use of Christian
phraseology and intellectual formularies which were not always
entirely necessary. But they never wavered on the basic element:
which was the necessity for complete tolerance for the expression
of religious belief. This was to be extended to any form of
heresy, not because heresy was to be welcomed but because
truth was not to be found, at the level where it needed to be
found, if men approached it from the wrong level. Men must be
free to be honestly wrong before they could be honestly right.

This particular problem is at the moment not a live issue,
though it might easily become one in an ideological war. But
there are certain aspects of the Quaker analysis which are as
relevant today as they were then. We are now agreed in our
tolerance of individual differences of religious belief: but what
of individual differences of action? Men may be permitted to
believe what they like; are they to be allowed to do what they
like?

The answer is to be found along the same lines as that of
belief. If the individual is to achieve full, responsible insight, he
must be free, and feel himself free, to express his insight in
whatever way seems to him to be right. Granted that there is a
plain difference between the works of the flesh and the fruits of
the spirit, it remains true that the fruits of the spirit are fruits,
to be 'grown' from a seed of understanding, and not works, to be
copied by external imitation. The tendency of a desire for moral
uniformity is towards the kind of hollowness of moral triviality
which Jesus found so deplorable in the scribes and Pharisees;
and the attempt to model ourselves by a set of rules or an
external example is stultifying to the inward growth of the
personality. 'The letter killeth, but the spirit giveth life.' Conduct
is a way of loving, and no external authority can lay down rules
to guide an individual in his way of loving.

There is, however, a service that can be rendered by one
man to another comparable to the 'testing' of experience by the
comparison of credal statements. Certain moral decisions may
be seen to follow from a certain experience, and they may be
elevated, not to condemn the individual who fails to perceive

their necessity, but to provide him with a guide to the development of his own moral insight. There is thus no means of determining the reality of a man's insight by measuring him against certain rules of conduct: whether he goes to church on Sundays, pays tithes, drives his car too fast, drinks beer, supports a measure of social reform, beats his wife. We could claim, I think, that a man who beat his wife was lacking in Christian insight in that particular matter, but we could not use this blind spot to test his whole spiritual condition. If we could, then we must surely be prepared to condemn as unchristian all members of the church who in the past accepted the institution of slavery, which the Christian conscience came in time to condemn. We cannot judge each other in this way, for though it might be possible to declare that a man who offended in a particular direction was not in possession of perfect moral insight (if there is any value in a declaration which must be true of all of us) we cannot, from any particular acts, decide on what might be described as 'the state of a man's soul'. Yet we must continue to believe that a fundamental unity of insight must express itself in a growing unity in action, and men may help each other to grow towards this external unity by making plain to each other the way they have been led in a particular direction.

Quakers have performed this process of moral illumination of each other, while at the same time guarding against the danger of setting up an external moral code, by a system of 'Advices and Queries', moral and spiritual reflections couched in the form most calculated to set the individual searching his own heart. When the earliest collection was put out, by certain responsible Friends, in 1656, they were set out not as regulations but as seeds of growth:

> Dearly beloved Friends, these things we do not lay upon you as a rule or form to walk by; but that all with a measure of the Light, which is pure and holy, may be guided; and so in the Light walking and abiding, these things may be fulfilled in the Spirit, not in the letter; for the letter killeth, but the Spirit giveth life.

The early Advices and Queries have been revised and extended, and the use of them continues the same, as a stimulus, a reminder, a challenge to thought and will. They are read at regular intervals in properly constituted meetings, whether for worship or business, so that once a year they may be 'kept before the members of our Religious Society'.

The Advice on education, to chose an example appropriate to the problem under discussion, reads thus:

> Seek for your children that full development of God's gifts which true education can bring. Remember that the service to which we are called needs healthy bodies, well-trained minds, high ideals and an understanding of the laws and purposes of God. Give of your best to the study of the Bible, and the understanding of the Christian faith. Be open minded, ready constantly to receive new light. Be zealous that education may be continued throughout life, and that its privileges may be shared by all.

And the corresponding Query runs:

> Are you striving to develop your mental powers and to use them to the glory of God? Are you loyal to the truth and do you keep your mind open to new light, from whatever quarter it may arise? Are you giving time and thought to the study of the Bible and other writings which reveal the ways of God?

The form of these two approaches is such as to draw the attention of members to the issue without laying down specific steps to be taken. The conscience can no longer be unaware of this particular field of intellectual and moral responsibility, though it may decide to ignore it. The Queries, indeed, were designed as questions-expecting-an-answer, but have become questions-to-provoke-thought – a reversion, this, to the true Quaker emphasis. A moral questionnaire smacks of external pharisaism; a challenge to turn inward and face the moral issues within the personality is genuine guidance-by-insight.

This extreme insistence on the necessity of moral, as of intellectual, freedom arises from the tender concern for the individual. In the end, only the individual matters: it is within his own life that each man must find salvation; and to this end some risks must be run. But complete anarchy defeats its own ends, for it sacrifices the many individuals for the one – and indeed, in practice, every genuine individual for the non-existent ideal of the one. Let there be freedom, for without it there can be no progress; but what happens when individuals betray their freedom? What when 'the light within thee be darkness'? What kind of social discipline may be exerted to defend the many, and the truth they seek to follow, from the darkness that can be raised by an evil will?

The essential principle is that if the will of God can be known to men, and a group of men are faithfully seeking to know it, they will ultimately agree. The whole procedure is thus based on the assumption that agreement is not only attainable, but ultimately certain; and that in arriving at agreement, all members of a meeting have their part to play. There is thus no provision for voting, which presumes the existence of a majority and minority view, and there is no chairman, with powers of discipline. Instead, every member may speak his mind, and one member, the Clerk, has the responsibility of gathering from the discussion what is the 'sense of the meeting', the elements upon which agreement has been reached. Every member has thus a measure of personal responsibility for the conduct of the meeting, and every member feels that the achievement of unity is his own concern. The Clerk is the servant of the group, to write a minute in response to the opinion of the group, and to submit it to the whole meeting for their correction until it represents the united will.

There is often controversy, and it is here that the strength of the Quaker method is most severely tested and most triumphantly displayed. The absence of a vote is a testimony to the belief that if men who disagree can wait humbly and faithfully they will learn in the fullness of time what is the will of God for them in that situation. To have a large majority on one side and a small group – or even one member – on the other does not mean that the will of God has become clear. There was a majority against Jesus when it was decided to crucify him. So as long as there is any member convinced that a proposed course of action is wrong, the meeting will wait for agreement. Naturally, there are frequent occasions, particularly when the matter is of no great importance, when the minority will have expressed its view, will find itself unable to convince the rest, and will itself then withdraw from the dispute, leaving the way clear for action, though perhaps itself remaining unconvinced. But whenever the matter is of real importance, a convinced minority can delay action until it has convinced the others, or been converted itself, or – and this is more likely, and usually more positive and creative – until a new solution has been found which preserves the conviction of all members.

What would normally be considered the chief drawback to this method is the possibility that it will be slow; and so it often is, maddeningly and sometimes harmfully slow. But Friends would reply that this is no fault of the method, but only of humanity. If men are slow to apprehend the will of God, they must be slow to act, for it is their business to act only in obedience. And there are certain clear advantages of the method, for though the decision may be slower to reach than if a vote had been taken and the will of the majority allowed to prevail, the achievement of unanimity is more rapid than by the normal procedure. This is because the fact that the goal is unity ensures that there will be no 'party lines' during the discussion. There may be two views, but the object of both 'sides' is to understand the view of the others and to make them understand theirs. There is thus no emotional rhetoric, no scoring of debating points, but a responsible, humble effort to

> proceed in the wisdom of God . . . not in the way of the world, as a world assembly of men, by hot contests, by seeking to outspeak and over-reach one another in discourse, as if it were controversy between party and party of men, or two sides violently striving for dominion . . . . not deciding affairs by the greater vote, or the number of men, . . . but . . . by hearing and determining every matter . . . in love, coolness, gentleness and dear unity.*

When a minority is outvoted in an ordinary democratic assembly on an issue which is felt to be of vital importance, there is inevitably an aftermath of bitterness, and a loss of social dynamic. In a healthy community there is a call for loyalty, and both 'sides' are expected to work vigorously according to the will of the majority. But though they may work loyally, they work with less energy and less devotion than they would have done for a policy that commanded their full approval. The Quaker policy of waiting for unity makes it possible for a line of action to be discovered that will call forth the complete dedication of all members.

This is true of decisions at the level of pure 'common sense'; but it is more excitingly true of the kind of decision that is reached after long waiting and seeking and seems to embody a new insight into the will of God. For it is by no means uncommon for a deadlock to arise, and a meeting to be bewildered and frustrated because two or more points of view are put forward obstinately and uncompromisingly; and then after intervals for reflection and further study and prayer – intervals perhaps of minutes, perhaps of months – for there to emerge a startling, overwhelmingly attractive solution that gathers up the threads of

*Edward Burrough.

the argument into a new pattern that transcends all that had gone before. And then, because there had been no 'parties' and no battlecries, and the members had not been forced by the exigencies of debate to commit themselves to a position from which there was no withdrawal, the way is at once open for the whole group to move into unity.

Another positive advantage of the delay involved in waiting for unanimity is that the resultant action has more chance of being radical, novel, contrary to the prejudices of the members. For when a totally new idea is presented to people, they tend to shrink from it; and if they were asked to vote on the issue as soon as it was introduced to them, they would turn it down. This is recognized in ordinary democratic practice, and the device of lobbying beforehand is intended to secure the necessary preparation. But lobbying is, after all, merely a method of discussion; and the Quaker method of settling all disputes in open, regulated discussion, takes up the practice of lobbying into its regular procedure. The new proposal is made; a majority is against it, but the minority is insistent; and the matter is discussed in all its aspects, and left over until unity can be reached. By the time the next meeting is held, the members have had time to accustom themselves to the startling idea, and have learnt to look at its face without wincing.

This truth is made abundantly clear by the common course of a Quaker discussion. When a new idea is presented, the usual practice is for the introduction of it to be followed by a period of silence, in which a stranger might suspect that the members are too stunned to respond, but which in fact represents an active mood of consideration. The first comments to be made may be foolish, or trite, or merely hostile; and the second and third perhaps take their cue from the first. But the clerk makes no move, and shows no signs of writing his minute. It is too early to be sure that these views represent the sense of the meeting; and the 'weighty' Friends have not yet spoken – for though quantity of opinion counts for little, quality counts for much, and those Friends who have consistently shown the fruits of wise thought and steady dedication are listened to with special readiness. Then the time comes when a Friend rises and speaks from the depth of his mind, with reflection that has had time to mature, and the discussion moves onto the deeper level of apprehension in which mere novelty is no bar to acceptance of an idea; in which the

spirit is humbled, detached from selfish and traditional con-
siderations by the realization that here are truths too great to be
easily grasped or easily rejected. There may then be a conflict of
opinion, or there may be merely a transfer of the whole argument
to this new level of understanding. In any case, the final words
are weighted with ripe wisdom and animated by a sense of
urgency. And now the clerk is busy. He has recognized the
authentic note, and he is struggling with the hard problems of
language, to find words which will carry the unexpected weight
they have to bear. At last he reads his minute to the meeting, and
after further contributions, which seek either to clarify the whole
issue further or merely to help the clerk in his task of record, he
produces an acceptable final version; and with murmurs of 'I
hope so', the matter is concluded.

These arrangements are often tedious in the extreme, but they
are less liable to 'go wrong' than the brisker, efficient methods of
handing over large spheres of responsibility to executive officers.
There are certain spheres in which this must be done: a head-
master must deal with certain problems as they arise, and the
medical superintendent of a mental hospital must have a large
amount of sheer, personal authority. Indeed the increase in
responsibility in such technical matters which has been rendered
necessary in late years, when medicine and education have become more incomprehensible to the layman, has presented the
Society with problems which it has not always solved in a spirit of
loving understanding. Other problems must be solved by the exercise of mere authority because there is not time to wait for unity
among the group at work together, as in bands of relief workers
during a war. But the Society is prepared to endure some dis-
comfort and to suffer some inefficiency in the steady pursuit of its
grand principle, and its own problems in this field are no more
serious than similar ones in public affairs, where the increasing
complication of technical problems of government has challenged
earlier preconceptions about the nature of democratic control.

The difficulty arises because there are frequently two ways of
solving a problem, either of which may be as 'good' as the other
in terms of human value, but which have differences that are
important in the narrow technical field. The problem is to
determine which are human values and which are matters of mere
technique. The question of which examinations a school should
offer is probably a technical one only; but the whole attitude of the

school to examinations is a human one. There is thus a wide field for differences of opinion and hurt feelings, and the Society of Friends has had its share of them all. But there can be no question of solving the problem by setting up a technical hierarchy with full executive authority.

This is but the modern form of the problems of authority that is always present, and the Quaker answer to the rival claims of priest and book is still relevant to the arrogance of the manager and the slide rule. As soon as Quakers step outside the general concerns of the whole group, into the kind of work which involves both technical and religious issues, they are faced by the same problems as face any human task in which personal relations and human values play a part, but accentuated for them by their belief that the human values matter more than technical efficiency. The difficulty may be illustrated from the problems of war-time relief, which was full of technical issues demanding expert knowledge, but the purpose of which was to express a corporate life which all the relief workers shared. Roger Wilson describes the situation in these words: *

When a plumber, an accountant, a nurse, a personnel manager, a cook, a telephone operator or the warden of an evacuation hostel are appointed by a private or public employer, they are appointed for specific duties and provided they fulfil those duties, their responsibility is ended. If they are good at getting on with other people, so much the better; if they quarrel with other people, they may have to go, however good they are at their technical job. But it is not ordinarily the business of any one of them as an employee to have views on how they shall all be co-ordinated, or on how the tasks shall be selected which, as an organization, they are to undertake. It is the job of the management to take responsibility for the general direction of the concern. A wise management will consult and inform subordinates and will attempt to draw them into policy making: it is no part of orthodox administrative theory that every member of the concern has equal moral responsibility for policy. But this is precisely where the F.R.S. was so different. Undertaking work 'under concern' means that the whole service is the Lord's and puts the Chairman, the General Secretary, the shorthand typist, the lorry-driver, the store keeper, the doctor and the accountant under an equal moral and spiritual commitment. And because as we recognize in the whole of our Quaker method of meeting for worship and for discipline, there is equality before the Lord, so there was an equality of responsibility in F.R.S.** which invalidated all orthodox conceptions of executive relationships. For in the work of the Lord the most junior member of the Service had a moral obligation to take

*Authority, Leadership and Concern.
**Friends' Relief Service.

8

responsibility for ends, and therefore for means, and unless he did take this responsibility the service ceased to express that part of its nature which was rooted in personal service under concern.

This method of operation demands a new conception of leadership. There must be leadership of a sort, but it must be leadership which sees whither the group is asking to be led.

> This means that the good Quaker leader, while not shirking his responsibility for giving a lead in virtue of his more extensive knowledge, must be very sensitive to any truer, even if less broadly based insights that can be drawn from his team-members. Acceptance of the truth from babes and sucklings is difficult to handle both administratively and emotionally. And to precisely the degree that the Quaker leader gives freedom for the initiative to come from others, he potentially weakens his own position as the issuer of instructions and the calculable negotiator with the outside world.

Quakers would not claim to have solved all the problems that this shared responsibility creates, but they have explored its difficulties and have seen enough of its triumph to provide them with an abiding faith in its value. They know something, in a favourite phrase, of the meaning of 'right ordering'. And what they know makes them certain that it can be transferred to the wider field of democratic government and even to international affairs. To quote Roger Wilson again:

> If democracy is to be capable of preserving creative freedom alongside the provision of adequate and ordered material existence for all, it must accept the tension between the moral equality which is basic to freedom and the hierarchy which is basic to orderly and dependable social organization. In major issues it is a terribly difficult tension to accept, and Christianity has done badly when it has offered men a prospect of escape from tension.

It is in the faithful acceptance of this tension, even at its costliest in time and personal commitment that Quakers have been most conscious of being drawn up from the dominance of their own wills into the knowledge of the will of God.

CHAPTER NINE

Worship

WE have seen in these last two chapters that man has two ways of preparing himself for the knowledge of God. The one, education in the widest sense of the equipment and dedication of mind, heart and will, represents man's search for reality. The other, the organization of fellowship in which each individual may feel the weight of his own responsibility and yet not be left to himself, represents the way in which the group may guide its members in their search. It is common in Christian thought to find both these man-made safeguards decried, as if it were to belittle the might of God and to set up man's puny intellect as a necessary protection against the overwhelming demands of the divine spirit; and in consequence there is suspicion of both learning and the guidance of the group. But there is no escape from either of them. Man must use his wits in the service of God; and he must be protected against the deceptive power of his own desires and the errors of his own mind.

These efforts of man's mind and will may be seen as ways of preparedness, of making ready, of finding places where we may be found. The man of learning is ready at more points than the man without, unless he has learned arrogance too, when he has opened his mind and closed his heart. And the member of a group who has learnt to listen to the guidance of the group is to that extent more ready, more accessible, more open.

But what can be said of the finding? What is the object of the guided search? This is something beyond the aid of learning, deeper than the guidance of the group. It is the recognition in the hidden centre of the personality of the worth, the worthship, the worship of God. It is to have sought for the secret of life, and to find it one of unfathomable awe and grandeur, greater than our pride or our possessions, greater than our pleasures or pains. It is to stumble on the discovery that the beauty of the hills and sea and stars, the heart-tendering power of humanity at its most loving and most lovely, the haunting sense that the mystery of life half reveals a destiny written for us alone, the dependence of children and old people, the dim perception of an unchanging moral law that lies beneath the shifts and devices of expediency – all these whisperings of aspiration are indeed the voices of a living universe, the messages of a Creator who, having set the world in motion, has not left it entirely at the mercy of its destructive impulses. This is a universal experience in worship, though the beliefs that spring from it may vary, for there runs through all religions the sense of being looked for by the spirit of the unseen, whether by gods or demons, angels or life-force.

And for the Christian the sense of being 'reached' is concentrated in his response to the story of Jesus of Nazareth, who seems to be himself a part of the whole effort of the universe to hold itself out to man; so that when he finds himself touched and humbled by this great, hardly perceptible reality, he recognises the touch and humbling power of the man Jesus. And so the two orders of reality come together: the ineffable, the transcendent, the numinous, the infinite, clad in glory, striding on the storm, beyond all knowledge and all account; and the clear, specific picture of the man who walked on a patch of earth and spoke to men like ourselves, wearing clothes that men had made, and concerned with problems of personal relations that press upon us to this day. This is the meaning of the 'divinity of Christ'; – not the intellectual acceptance of a statement of relationship between one divine being and another, but the discovery that the universe, vague, intangible, is active in love, and that as it touches us, its impact on our heart and will is of the same order as the impact of Jesus. We cannot conceive of being loved by the universe, and yet that is what it seems to be; and we come to see the meaning of this vague, indescribable impression when we see the life of one who was supremely conscious of being loved by the Father of the universe; and not only being loved, but being 'loved through'.

We worship God when we see this kind of worth in him, and respond to it in an outflowing of feeling from the depths of our personality. We are convinced for the moment – however much other interests may deflect our attention at other times – that here we are in contact with the central reality; that this, above all things, is what life is for. 'Master, it is good for us to be here,' said Peter on the Mount of the Transfiguration; and there is the same sense of finality, of being for the moment where man ought to be, at the heart of all worship.

Now it is this that man sets out to find. This is the source of light for which he dedicates his mind and curbs his will. His education and his discipline are nothing more than ways of preparation for worship, of making himself ready to be overwhelmed by the worth of God, as a walk in the country is a preparation for the experience of natural beauty. And it has been found necessary, too, to make another kind of preparation, in the arrangement of times and places when other distractions will be set aside, and men will turn deliberately to an *act* of worship. The experience of worship may occur at any time, and in any place; and unexpectedly

> The drift of pinions, would we hearken,
> Beats at our own clay-shuttered doors.*

But though God is not to be hindered in his search for man, it is a truth of experience that the act of worship, the deliberate organization of an opportunity for deepening awareness of the 'worth' of God, is a prime necessity for the growth into light. It has been common in the history of Christianity for a set form to be used, so that a familiar loveliness might recall the mind from its wandering attention and direct it to the centre of all life. The highest form of worship the church has used is the Eucharist, with its long history, its fundamental simplicity combined with the possibility of immense complexity according to special needs, and its power of holding a number of different elements in a single, unified experience. There is here music that can set vibrating all the chords of the Christian experience, as the ritual, stately or intimate in different circumstances, moves through its themes: the recalling of the law, and the unchanging moral principle implied by a belief in one God; the lessons from the New Testament, speaking as the year turns of the great events and ideals of the early Christian story; the prayer for the church and the confession, drawing worshippers into the humble selflessness which allows the life from without to break in; then the slow approach to the central mystery itself, a mystery unfathomably clothed in the common symbol of a meal, evoking with but little aid from language the community, the oneness, of men in their dependence on the source of life; and finally the committal of

ourselves, our souls and bodies, to be a reasonable holy, and lively sacrifice unto thee,

*F. Thompson, *The Kingdom of God*.

with the prayer that

> we may continue in that holy fellowship, and do all such good works
> as thou hast prepared for us to walk in;

and the great hymn of glory, the singing of the heart as it flows
out in love and adoration.

In the lovely dignity of the language and the solemn power of
the unchanging ritual there is a means to catch the attention and
to entangle the thoughts and mind and body, to hold the externals
of life in an attitude which the inward spirit may copy, and so
traffic in the depths with the spirit of God. Because of its supreme
all-embracingness, the service has been used for all the central
acts of worship individual and corporate: for crowning a king or
ordaining a priest, for marriage and requiem; and for a single
worshipper to bring his own griefs or perplexities or conflicts and
face them in the presence of one who took a meal with his friends
before he went out to Gethsemane. At these special times the
time-honoured form takes on a peculiar poignancy, as God himself seems closest when human life is at one of its most testing
and revealing moments.

It is a sign of the radical nature of the early Quaker experience
that despite the beauty and power of this central Christian liturgy
it was abandoned by Friends and replaced by silence. This was
done, however, in no spirit of protest or negativism, but in an
attempt to assert positively the values which the Eucharist itself
had sought to assert, but which at the time were being neglected.
The object of a ritual is ultimately to secure a quiet heart and
mind, to which God may speak: to still the wandering thoughts
which would otherwise turn to the vexations and hopes and
aspirations which are the common stuff of daily life, and to turn
them to the one great theme. The sounds and sights of ritual
are a making ready for stillness, an entangling of the senses in
the spiritual business of worship.

But if that is so, it follows that if the ritual leads to a noisy
heart instead of a quiet one, it has failed of its purpose. And at
the time of the Quaker origins, the Eucharist was the centre of
ecclesiastical argument and the very focus of controversy. At a
time when one could not attend a communion service without
being reminded of bitter debate it was appropriate to ask, Was
this form, for all its acknowledged value in the past, a necessity
for all men and for all time? And the Quaker, searching out all

the implications of his belief that God dealt with man in the inwardness of his own heart, was convinced that it was not necessary. So he rejected the set form, which for the time being was a hindrance, and claimed to know God without it. God was not limited by his own means; and even if the Eucharist had been divinely instituted (which he was inclined to doubt) that did not mean that God could be approached in no other way. Friends thus rejected all predetermined forms of worship, mass and liturgy, hymn and psalm, and instead made their meetings of silence, with speech coming only from an inward compulsion.

And to this day, if anyone strays into a Quaker meeting, he will find that the framework of it consists of stillness, from which speech rises from time to time and into which it returns. It is noticeably an active silence, not a mere absence of sound, but a sensible tautness, a mood of expectancy, of waiting for something to happen, and of being bent towards the source of the event; an air of poised watchfulness, utterly distinct from dreamy reverie, a certain tension that draws out the mind and heart, stilling the vague eddies of normal anxiety, dissipating transient, personal desires, and seeming to turn the face in a new direction, to orientate the personality, in the full, original sense of that word.

This stark emptiness arose at a time when the fullness of ritual was a barrier to insight; but it remains of positive value even now, when the bitterness of conflict over the Eucharist has died down and the argument, where it survives, is conducted in the hopes of unity rather than the hopes of difference; for there is still a need to be reminded that God is not limited by his own means. It is always possible to enjoy a ritual for the wrong reasons and not know that one has missed the secret: to be moved by beauty and miss the beauty of holiness, to feed on language and miss the message. But if a man sits in silence with other worshippers, and nothing happens, he knows that nothing has happened. If the means to worship are rich and lovely, we can mistake the means for the reality; but if the means are nothing and the worship all, then we cannot miss the worship without knowing what we have lost. We must meet the truth, or we meet nothing.

But though the silence is thus the framework and climax of worship, men need each other's expressed support if they are to use it positively, and not merely sit in emptiness of mind. Quakers have thus made use of a vocal ministry, as a means of raising the meeting to the common level of awareness which is needed. This ministry is free and unplanned, for as 'the wind bloweth where it listeth', so the message of God may come unexpectedly to one who was not consciously prepared for it. Howard Brinton describes the practice thus:

> The theory of the Quaker ministry is simple. As the worshippers sit together in silence to wait upon the Lord, anyone among them may find arising in his consciousness a message which he feels is intended for more than himself alone. It is then his obligation to deliver that message and to cease speaking when he has delivered it. He must learn to recognize the unique sense of urgency which is evidence of a divine requirement . . There is no sure test of divine guidance in this or any other undertaking. If, however, through prayer and humble waiting he has become sensitive to the 'still, small voice', he will be increasingly enabled to recognize a call when it comes.°

The best spoken ministry is of this kind, arising from the meeting itself rather than from previous preparation, taking, it seems, the minister himself by surprise as much as the rest of the group. Practised Friends are accustomed to this unexpectedness, the sense of being used by a truth that they have not sought for; but to the beginner the whole experience is alarming and humbling. The point is well made in an article by Howard Hayes, 'On speaking at a Quaker meeting'.°°

> As a newcomer to a Quaker Meeting, I found it pleasant to sit quietly, to experience the novel effect of the silence, and then to listen passively while perhaps towards the end of the hour someone spoke. The 'performance', if you could call it that, seemed to be a fresh and original invention. New and yet, I realised, very old; simple, yet strangely mysterious.
> I knew that a long time ago Quakers actually quaked. A spirit got into them and shook them . . But that was a long way back in history. Today, no one quaked. The modern, enlightened person could afford no such lack of control over his feelings . . .
> Sometimes an almost dreamlike quality seemed to hang over our little Meeting. Undoubtedly, as the weeks went by, we were rolling up an excellent collection of meditative hours together. Like the 'arches of the years' I could see these meditative hours reaching back into the past and forward into the future in simple identity and repetition.
> Much of the speaking was not very different from good reading. In fact, it was good reading of the calm and serious kind. It did not disturb the peaceful, meditative mood of the morning, and one could sit and watch the gentle swirling of the dust in the sunbeams without any serious internal disturbances.
> Perhaps this was what one really wanted. Was this all there was to it?

°*Friends for 300 Years.*
°°*Friends Intelligencer.*

This timeless calm, this respite of peace, this slow deep breathing, this wordless proximity to others for an hour—should one bother one's head for anything more?

Oddly enough, too, there was nothing soporific about it. We were far removed from sleep. On the contrary, the removal of outward distractions seemed to produce a high and special form of wakefulness.

The sleeping pool of one's mind came slowly and clearly into view. Its usual mists had lifted. The occasional criss-crossing of ripples did not disturb. There was a waiting, and expectancy, but time seemed to have lost its usual value and measurements. Now and then it disappeared entirely.

One or two persons had spoken. Perhaps they were the ripples. But they had left a slight potential in the air. And then a person got up whom I had not heard before. Something that had been said had touched him off. A few words, perhaps, a mere pinpoint of religious truth, but it had set off something within him. He was not visibly quaking, but one quickly sensed that he was disturbed at a far deeper level than those who had gone before. A new region had been lighted up.

As he spoke I began to quake. That was the simple fact of the matter. And it took me as much by surprise as if I had been stabbed. My breathing changed, my heart began to pound, my very breastbone was invaded by this quaking. These are distressing sensations.

They were the more inexplicable as I was in a position of complete anonymity. Nothing was expected of me. Nobody was looking at me, no one would turn to me to say: 'You're next.' I had no 'duty' to perform. I was only one of a quietly gathered group.

Yet in the end I had no choice. Here was something very difficult to argue with, though argue with it I did. The situation was as if I had been let down suddenly on the back of a galloping horse, with the reins shoved in my hand and no further instructions. Protesting that I was not a horseman did no good. And not being a horseman in such a spot produces more fear than joy.

There had been some silence, and then I arose and spoke, quaking throughout. What I said I don't know, and it wasn't recorded. Afterwards I sat down, still quaking. Slowly I reined in the galloping beast, slipped to earth, and caught my breath. Somehow I had skinned through safely. I noted that all was calm around me. The silence was resumed as before. No windows were broken. The dust particles were still slowly turning in the sunbeams falling over the ancient benches. The Elders sat as solidly and meditatively as they always did. If there had been an earthquake, as it had seemed to me, no damage was visible and no one had been seriously shaken up. I heaved a vast sigh of relief.

Only later (in my egotism) did it occur to me that I had added nothing more than a small mite to what had been set going by others and kept going by them. With all my quaking I had contributed no more than a few words to the group sermon that had mysteriously flowered out of that silent morning hour.

The phrase 'group sermon' is apt for the total impression of Quaker ministry. Sometimes one individual's contribution will be recognizably prepared, sometimes profitably, when hard study of a passage of the Bible will yield spiritual insight that could be obtained in no other way; sometimes harmfully, or at least unprofitably, when the prepared message, though good enough in its way, does not seem to fit. It is this fitness that is all: the inter-play of minds and hearts, the readiness to speak to another's condition, to meet as one can the need of others gathered there expectant, and to be used mysteriously for the purpose of God for the whole group. Penn challenged his readers to search their hearts in this matter, and to find out if they came to give of their own store or to be used for another's:

> When you come to your meetings . . . . what do you do? Do you then gather together bodily only, and kindle a fire, compassing yourselves about with the sparks of your own kindling, and so please yourselves, and walk in the 'Light of your own fire and the sparks which you have kindled'? Or rather, do you sit down in True Silence, resting from your own Will and Workings, and waiting upon the Lord, with your minds fixed in that Light wherewith Christ has enlightened you, until the Lord breathes life in you, refresheth you, and prepares you, . . that you may offer unto him a pure and spiritual sacrifice?[*]

This reliance on the initiative of God, on being touched and used by a message instead of bringing one ready made, does not imply that the speaker is an entirely passive agent. The same con-siderations apply here, to the problem of preparation for speaking in a meeting for worship as apply to education for insight. The object of preparation is readiness, availability to the truth; and the kind of preparation which is most relevant is not the specific organization of reflections about a spiritual problem, but the slow, general development of insight and understanding of the spiritual isues with which daily life is beset. The speaker brings into the meeting for worship the fruits of his spiritual struggle and the sen-sitiveness he has learnt in life. There is a danger in the elaborate, purposeful preparation that may tempt a man into speaking too easily, and with too little regard to the needs of the moment. He may offer what Barclay called 'conned and gathered stuff', or as other Friends said, he may be 'grinding with the water that is passed'. The object of all ministry is, said Fox, to bring people to the end of all preaching, and as to 'minister' is to serve, so will ministry serve the living experience.

In a meeting for worship where the life rises in this way, there

[*] *A Tender Visitation.*

is usually to be met something of the same variety and richness
of experience that is symbolized and provoked by the Eucharist.
The external reminders are absent, but the inward reality is the
same: the senses are dealt with differently, but the spirit grapples
with the same influences; and it is no mere trick with words to
claim, as Quaker writers do, that the doctrine of the Real Presence
has its own application to silent worship. Indeed, the very rhythm
of worship is often closely similar to that of the Eucharist: first
the impact of the silence itself, a sudden hush as the worshipper
steps out of the noisy street and meets in it the challenge of the
law and unchangeable facts of history and Christian experience,
as in the Decalogue and the Epistle and Gospel. Then the time
of 'settling', familiar to all live meetings, in which it is rare for
words to be spoken, except perhaps for a simple offering of prayer,
a time in which the individual has to deal with the problems of
his own self-consciousness, his wandering thoughts, his sense of
unworthiness, the recollection of failure, the anxieties that spring
from his lack of understanding and assurance. Then the meeting
seems to progress, often with the assistance of spoken ministry,
the silent flowering of meditation, or the march towards the
resolution of a spiritual tension arising from a perplexity or doubt.
And then, towards the end, a turning outwards of loving tenderness towards the world into which the worshippers must soon
return, prayerful concern for families, friends, and out further to
a care for 'all men everywhere', as Friends are fond of saying, a
care too vague to hold in the mind or heart, but in an inexplicable
manner held, as it were, between the individual and the living
God. This progress is usually made beneath the surface, though
signs of it rise like ocean islands from time to time and break the
stillness, showing through in words the result of what has gone
on deeper than words can reach.

But there is a deeper resemblance than this between the silent
worship and the underlying meaning of the Eucharist. The
historic ritual expresses the way in which the Christian finds that
a growing knowledge of God heightens his value for man. Put in
terms of mere logic it might be said that if God is our common
Father, then we are all brothers. And that is true as far as it goes;
but even in human relationships, it is still possible to quarrel with
one's brother, despite the plain fact of a common fatherhood.
Such argument is irrelevant to the springs of human conduct: it
is on the wrong level. But if the knowledge of God as a father

becomes a matter of urgent, personal experience, then the brotherhood of man becomes a matter of experience too, as brothers learn to love each other better in a family where parents and children are in sympathy with each other. As the radii of a circle approach the centre, they draw nearer to each other; and as divided souls seek deeper into the source of life, they find each other close in understanding and interdependence.

There are thus two, fused elements in the experience of worship; communion with God and fellowship with other worshippers. And as the communion service has symbolized this truth throughout the years, so Friends have spoken to its reality. Fox, writing in 1655, testified to it:

> In all your Meetings know and feel the Power, and the Seeds . . . . of the Lord God amongst you, over you, and in you; then in that ye will feel the Presence of the Lord God dwelling in the midst of you. And to the Lord your Hearts will be brought, and it will bring you nigh one to another, and to come into sweet Love and Unity, and into Easiness and Open-ness of Heart; and keep you over all that which would stain you, or hurt you, or defile you.[°]

And again, in his next epistle:

> All Friends every where, Keep your Meetings, waiting in the Light, which from the Lord Jesus Christ doth come; so will ye receive Power from Him, and have the refreshing Springs of Life opened to your Souls, and be kept sensible of the tender Mercies of the Lord. And know one another in the Life (ye that be turned to the Light) and in the Power, which comes from the Lord Jesus Christ . . . . [°°]

'Know one another in the Life' – this was a phrase that was to echo through Quaker admonition; and later Friends were to speak in their own way of the same experience. Samuel Fothergill writes of [°°°]

> cool moments of sedate meditation when the mind is loosened from lower connections . . . reaching onwards to the immutable union and inseparable fellowship of the Lord's family.

And Howard Brinton, in 1952, reports the same thing: [°°°°]

> He whose soul is irradiated by the Light of Christ is in union with God and his fellows.

[°] *Epistle 104.*
[°°] *Epistle 105.*
[°°°] *Memoirs and Letters.*
[°°°°] *op. cit.*

The one is the source, the other the measure, of the growing life in God: the one, union with God, the sense that here the spirit is alone with its destiny, facing the ultimate mysteries of life, and overwhelmed with the glory that confronts it. 'My mind,' said John Woolman, 'was covered with an awefulness.' And on the other hand, the assurance that even here, on the fringes of human knowledge, we are not alone, but are closer than we knew to men and women whose needs, superficially different, are here in the depths the same.

And when this fusion of souls has taken place, there flows from it a new desire to hold all life in the same unity, and to know communion and fellowship in the commonplace as it has been known in the mysterious. One of the positive elements in the apparently negative attitude to sacraments is that particular sacraments are denied so that all things may be sacramental. There is no holy meal because all meals are holy, no moment of baptism because all growth toward God provides forgiveness and renewal, no sacramental marriage ceremony because the shared life is itself the expression of Christian love, no oaths because all speech is sacred to honesty, no raising of hats because all personal relations are filled by the courtesy of Christ. This principle, of a denial that is an assertion of the inwardness of reality, runs through all Quaker thought and practice, and is focussed in the meeting for worship and its fruits in daily life. There is no sacred ministry because all men are ordained to be vessels of the truth: and no special forms, because the worth of God is to be responded to wherever it may be seen. Thus, though the necessity of meeting in the flesh for times of worship is agreed on all sides, it is usual for moments of worship to arise spontaneously in odd places and at odd times: in a living room when a group would be sitting talking, and

> one member might be discovered to be sitting in silence with a look of solemnity on his face. The whole group would gradually become silent. After a time, the person whose attitude of worship had initiated the meeting would, in all probability, convey a message which he had on his mind. A period of silence would ensue, after which the general conversation would be resumed.*

And beyond this sustained expectancy of times of living silence goes the hope that all that is done, all personal relations, all deeds and words, all thought and work and life, may be touched with

*Brinton, *op. cit.*

the same spirit as the act of worship itself. This is orthodox Christianity, and Quakers are here in no way peculiar. But it is to be expected that the peculiarity of the emphasis and method will involve certain special emphasis in the sacramental life itself. There are some 'concerns' that are specially dear to them, some points of conflict in the moral sphere that they pay particular attention to. To these peculiarities we must now turn; but they will not be understood unless it is remembered that they arise, not from logical deductions from doctrine, but from a whole attitude of personality that is developed in the meeting for worship. The young lover who goes about meeting reminders of his love at every turn is not making logical deductions: and the Christian who finds himself turned heart and mind towards a God who comes in the silence to meet him does not go out to love the other children of the Father with the love of deductive reason. There is logic in it, but it is the logic of the heart.

CHAPTER TEN

Creative Love: Personal Relationships

UP to this point I have been concerned with the individual interpretation of the meaning of human life: what is man? how can he meet the reality that he hungers for? Or to put it in terms of the answer rather than the question, I have been trying to interpret the great commandment, Thou shalt love the Lord thy God. But this commandment has never stood by itself, and living Christian experience has never for long found joy in the love of God without finding itself involved in the love of man: Thou shalt love thy neighbour as thyself. Wherever the seed has taken root, it has been fruitful, with a fruit that is the recognizable product of the seed.

In emphasizing the close connexion between experience and action, between the love of God and the love of man, between the spirit and the fruits of the spirit, Quakerism has but expressed the universal Christian experience. The Franciscan emphasis on the fact that to find one's heart touched by the love of God means also that one's heart turns outwards in the love of God's children is an essential element in catholic Christianity. But as Quakerism came into being in an attempt to emphasize a particular element in man's relationship with God, it found itself also with a particular emphasis to lay on man's relationship with man. We have seen that the doctrine of the inner light placed on each individual the responsibility of turning to God and accepting the divine charge for himself. When all that may be has been learnt from sacred books and men speaking with authority, the crowning element in the search is the moment when in the depths of his personality the seeker finds himself as it were face to face with God, alone, naked, with a burden of choice that he cannot share — and a flash of joy that he would not share. This capacity for a meeting with God is the most significant of man's powers: it is what man is for.

And as that is true of the life of the individual, in and for himself, it is also true of the other men with whom he has to deal.

They are important not because they provide pleasant company, or because they are a potential threat to his own comfort or standard of living, or because they are amusing or disgusting, or because they hold high rank in society. They are important for one thing: their capacity for meeting with God. And as that is the source of their significance, it is the point of contact between man and man. True human fellowship rests on this shared divinity, not on our shared humanity. We belong to each other not because we have the same need of food and shelter, security and affection, but because each of us belongs to God.

Here again, there is no great originality in the Quaker position, which could be matched by many statements of the meaning of Christian brotherhood. The originality lies simply in this: that Quakers have tried to behave as if this concept of brotherhood had already come true in practice, and to treat with other men as if they had already embraced the authority of divine love. It was this that was the radical element in the early Quaker witness. At a time when warring sects were striving to secure a position of authority so that they should be able to lead the nation into the paths of righteousness (for that is the motive they would have given for their struggle) Friends began to behave as if no such authority were necessary. Instead of waiting until their enemies had become friends before extending their love to them, they began to love their enemies as if they were friends already, speaking to 'that of God in them' instead of to the motives of fear and prudence. And they did not merely speak in words but in deeds, trusting their own lives and property to this same potential knowledge of God with no defence but the armour of God. In the event, they suffered for their trustfulness: they lost their property and they themselves were hustled into gaol; but their faith never flagged. They believed that if they continued to speak to the godlike part of evil men, then the godlike part would be the more able to deal with the evil,

> that by bringing them to something that was of God in themselves, they might the better know and judge of Him and themselves.*

Normally human relations are conducted on a dual basis: we have one standard of behaviour for our friends and relatives (the in-group of the anthropologists) and another for the people we are compelled to have dealings with for business or other reasons

*Penn's preface to Fox's *Journal*.

(the out-group). The in-group we deal with, broadly, on a basis of love, co-operation and unselfishness. We usually like each other, or have come to accept each other as people with a claim on our services. We have a measure of common understanding, and we tolerate each other's oddities and failings, up to a point, because we attach a value to a whole personal relationship.

We tend to approach the out-group on a basis of a potential conflict. We deal with a man in the way of business, and we try to obtain the highest value for our goods and the lowest value for his. We meet someone who wants to get on the same train as we do, and we make as certain as possible of getting on before he does. We work alongside someone in the same office, and unless a friendship strikes up, and we take him into the in-group, we regard him in some measure as our rival in the struggle for promotion. In practice, this conflict is controlled by custom and law, so that we may by right indulge certain of our desires and are compelled to forego other desires in return. We resign the right to drive on one side of the road in the hope of finding our side free from opposing traffic. We form a queue for a bus, and thus resign the hope of getting on first in return for a guarantee that we shall not be always last.

The Christian judgement on this distinction between the in-group and the out-group has always been that there was, in the eyes of God, no such thing. All men are children of God, and to the Christian all men are members of the in-group. But in practice this has usually meant that the Church sought to bring all men into fellowship, and not, commonly, to treat them all as if they already were. This is the distinction between the Quaker position and the general tendency of organized Christianity. The church has defended its position on grounds of a preparatory phase, a stage in history when the rule of law must prevail until men are ready for the rule of love, as children must obey their parents until they are able to judge for themselves, or as the Jews were subject to the laws of Moses until the new covenant of the love of Christ. The work of the church might thus be defined as the acceptance of law and justice, the education of imperfect men and the preparation for a rule of love.

This position the early Quakers wholeheartedly rejected. Their challenge to the whole concept of conflict in human affairs was first made explicit in the rejection of war – and it is this particular manner of testifying that remains their most distinctive mark.

9

But the early Friends were not content with rejecting war: they embraced a new relationship with other men that rejected conflict. They believed that if an enemy were to be treated as an enemy, he would remain one for ever; if he were to be treated as a friend, he might become one. Or to put it in language they would have preferred to use, if we appeal to that of God in other men, there is a possibility that the appeal will be heard, and the voice of God in the heart will be obeyed more readily; but if we appeal to that of the devil, it will be the devil who will be obeyed. Hate, hostility, suspicion, even prudence, are all negative, and produce hate, hostility, suspicion, prudence. Love, friendliness, trustfulness, recklessness can reach out in the most unpromising circumstances and arouse their like.

They do not always succeed, but it is not success that is the mark of Christian obedience: it is obedience. The object of living is not security (which merely means going on living) but the showing of love, the effort to establish contact with 'that of God' in other men. If this is so, there is almost something to be welcomed in a difficult or hostile situation, for it is there that love has most to do, the greatest opportunity. Love gains its greatest triumphs over the blackest hate, not when it merely flows out in response to love itself.

> For if ye love them that love you, what reward have ye?
> Do not even the publicans the same?

It was in the spirit of these words of Jesus that a Quaker once replied to an objector who argued that he would be prepared to follow the way of peace when other men were of the same mind:

> So then thou hast a mind to be the last man to be good. I have a mind to be one of the first and set the rest an example.*

And in the same spirit Howard Brinton writes:

> We are not commanded to love our enemies only when there are no enemies, nor to overcome evil with good only when there is no evil.**

There is a clear issue here that has often been confused by a difference of opinion over the meaning of the word 'love'. If love means liking, the commandment to love our neighbour as ourselves becomes meaningless, for it is plainly impossible to 'like' all men equally. And as soon as the definition of love is pressed beyond this common, daily usage of attraction, it is possible to

*John Hoag, *Journal*.
**Friends for 300 years.*

make it imply all kinds of odd behaviour : the punishment of offenders as a means to their moral improvement, the torture of heretics as a means to their eternal salvation, euthanasia as a means of relieving pain. What, then, in practice has the word come to imply? How have Quakers sought to love their neighbours, and to appeal to that of God in every man?

The essential principle, it will be recalled, is the element of godlikeness in all men, the capacity for meeting with God, the power of responding to the light. It is for this potential, and not for his achievement in other ways, that a man is valued in the sight of God. It therefore follows that all men will be 'equal', and will be regarded as equal, in their most significant element. The whole problem of human equality is so difficult, and has taken such strange forms in this day of its triumph – to the extent of pretending that men are equal in ways that they are patently not so – that this corollary of the doctrine of the inner light is open to some misunderstanding. The nearest analogy is that of the family, in which the clever child is enjoyed for his cleverness, but gains no status from it, no special share of cake, or maternal affection, in reward for his intellect. The dull child *matters* as much as the bright. Among Friends, the system of open meetings provides the opportunity for each member of the society to make his own contribution, without regard to his outward standing, and in terms of opportunity of service and personal value each member matters as much as another.

The same principle is applied in ordinary human relations outside the group. The humble, apparently insignificant person matters as much as the important one, the poor as much as the wealthy. In the past, this witness to the significance of every man took the form of the rejection of current modes of politeness – the distinction in address between thou and thee, hat-honour, and all the rest. In modern times the Quaker is not so easily recognizable by any difference in this matter because the battle has been largely won. If there is as much snobbery as ever (as some would argue) it is a silent, unconfessed snobbery. All men are addressed, not as 'thou', but as 'you'. Hat-honour is extended, not to the mighty, but to all – or, in the present careless generation, to none. And if 'your grace' still echoes comfortingly in the ears of the holder of the title, it is only to him that it has any significance at all.

If there is any need for the continued Quaker witness in this matter, it is not in the rapidly crumbling edifice of rank based on inheritance or wealth, but in the distinction to which, in a technological age, the various 'experts' lay claim. With specialization as the very condition of our survival, we need to know from some external sign whether or not a man's technical judgement may be respected – whether a doctor is 'qualified' to prescribe for us or no. And while this is undeniably necessary, we are fast approaching the point at which qualifications will matter more than worth, a degree or a diploma more than knowledge and skill. And more than that, the expert in one sphere tends to speak with authority, and be heard as if he had authority, in another. The danger of this is inherent in the situation; but it may be guarded against by an insistence on the value of persons *as persons*, not merely in theory, but in the living practice of community. This may still be found among Friends, who are still often thought unnecessarily blunt and brusque, or forgetful of the graces of life, because they fail to pay respect to the external marks of learning, or because they will listen patiently and hopefully to a fool. No more than others are they prone to accept the folly of the fool, but they listen and sift it and give it its chance.

As a means to this kind of respect for personality as such, Quakers have also sought to live plainly, without asceticism but without display. In time this plainness came to be sustained as part of an economic witness, but in the beginning it was more direct, the simple recognition that men could not be conscious of their equality if one were to look grander and more impressive than the other. Early Friends were scoffed at for paying attention to such trivialities as the decorations of dress, for preaching down 'ribbons and lace and points and cuffs', but they were the marks of the gentleman; and Quakerism sought to ignore the marks of the gentleman in looking for true gentleness. Again, this particular battle has been largely won, and Quaker grey has passed into history. And though differences in wealth continue, they are not now so important. Pride in riches is no longer a serious spiritual issue.

One aspect of the early Quaker witness to the value of every personality which has taken on greater importance with the passage of time is the relationship between the sexes. From the earliest days, women Friends were free to make exactly the same contribution, to speak and be listened to, to serve and to lead, as men. There were at one time separate meetings for women, but that was a mere recognition of what will always be to some extent true, that women have some interests, as women, which are different from men's. In the course of time, the women's meetings disappeared, and now there is no distinction of sex whatever. Women speak in meeting for worship, sit on committees, make plans and carry them out, in full partnership with the men of the Society.

This was not a problem to which Quakers have ever addressed much attention, and they have never led a suffragette crusade. But they achieved without thinking about it a relationship between the sexes which the organized denominations have not achieved yet, and which the secular world had to buy with much suffering and bitterness. Indeed they attained more, for the Quaker concept has remained throughout that of a partnership. There was never any talk of 'emancipation', for it was not desired that women should be 'free' of men, but that they should be their partners. And while the western world has seen the dawn of 'emancipation', it has lost even what partnership there was. The swelling tide of divorce and matrimonial tension arises from the discovery that the sexes may now become 'free' of each other, and the loss of the old loyalty to the idea of partnership. There can never be any going back, for nobody would have us return to a partnership in which one partner was the senior by the mere fact of sex; but there is urgent need to go on to the free, loving partnership of voluntary co-operation. The following 'Counsel as to marriage' represents the ideal of the Society:

> Marriage is an ordinance of God, appointed for the help and blessing of both man and woman, and for the right up-bringing of the next generation . . The union of husband and wife is therefore fraught with momentous issues, and is not to be thought of lightly. Happiness and blessing in marriage depend first on the presence of devoted love, a love which is not the outcome of a merely passing attraction, but which includes a real respect by each for the personality of the other. Every such union should be undertaken in the fear of the Lord, and with a reverent attention to His counsel and guidance. It will be owned and blessed by Him if the healthy love that draws two human souls together is sanctified by the larger love of Christ and of His brethren; it will yield its fairest fruit as it is chastened by the discipline of care and trial bravely borne, and ripened into self-forgetting devotion by the mutual influence of parents and children. The family is the standing witness that man is not intended to live alone: that he becomes what he is meant to be as his character is trained in unselfishness by responsibility for others, and by the claims and duties of a common life.°

°*Christian Practice.*

This, it might be argued, is but an ideal, a counsel of perfection; but it is a counsel based on experience. It is not an accident when marriages succeed; their success is the result of a certain definite attitude in regarding marriage as an opportunity of giving rather than getting. Most marriages start with this condition – young lovers indulging in sweet rivalry to anticipate each other's wants, to eat the smaller piece of cake, and to carry the larger share of the burden. But this desire to give often fades when the partners become 'sure' of each other, and there is no need to win each other's love. It is then that they lose each other, when their first unselfishness loses its selfish purpose, when there is nothing to be gained by giving. It is at this point that the marriages that succeed have done so because they were sustained by a higher purpose than gratification, an object greater than the moment. It is now that children may be of value, in making their inescapable demands on their parents, and joining them in an alliance of service and care. And it is here, too, that the Christian experience is most relevant – and is known to be so by Christian couples – holding a pair together in the knowledge that though they have both of them faults and imperfections they belong together to God.

> Those marriages in which God, who is love, has joined husband and wife together, are the most likely to endure and to grow more beautiful with the passage of years,

continues the Quaker counsel; and this is the plain truth, not only in the fallible experience of ordinary observation, but even to the dry, if insensitive eye of scientific research. If a couple live together for their own amusement, then as soon as their amusement begins to pall, it would seem sensible to part, and seek fresh dalliance elsewhere. But if they are joined as their way of sharing in a large destiny, they can endure the boredom and drudgery and revulsions of feeling that occur in all long tasks – becoming an artist, or learning to play cricket, or learning to love each other – until the day comes when they have their reward – being an artist, or playing cricket, or loving each other. None of these things comes 'by nature', for though in all of them some of us are better than others they must all be won by practice and devotion and growing old in faithfulness. The words of counsel continue, on this point:

> The enduring tie is essential, in order to secure to the children their right to a settled home, and to the care and distinctive influence of both

father and mother; it is also necessary to the well-being of society as a whole.

Since these words were written in 1925, every point in them has been brought home to us in the fierce illumination of war: the increase in divorce and the sure consequence in increase in child-misery, with its outlet in delinquency and neurosis; the absence of fathers from home, and the special losses to the young that have followed on them; and, though our social ills are too com-plex to be traced to this, or any other one cause, the 'well-being of society' has plainly lost by the decline in marriage. The sexual 'freedom' of our time has left us not less inhibited, but more, tormented by a search for satisfaction that is never found.

Lust is no new device, discovered by our generation; but we have our own refinements of stimulation, and we are laying ourselves open to temptation in a peculiarly efficient and reckless manner. We have come to deplore what we fancy was the dangerously hush-hush attitude of our grandparents, but we are guilty of the same error in proportion when we thrust sexual interests to the foreground, and fail to 'contain' them in our whole spiritual growth. For lust is the desire of the body without the soul, as repression was the desire of the soul without the body. And if repression carried the possibility of disaster, licence carries its certainty. Friends were perhaps thinking more of our grand-parents when they wrote their counsel in 1925, but their words are applicable to the new situation too:

> We believe that unthinking fear of the sex instinct is a cause of much harm, and that the moral difficulties connected with sex often arise from ignorance or from one-sided knowledge communicated through impure channels. We cannot think that God has implanted in us this powerful and deep rooted instinct, without intending it to be used for our help in our upward climb. If our conception of it can be enlarged and ennobled we ought to be able to transmute its power into the realisation and achievement of a full and useful life; and in so doing it may be given to us to help others who are in some danger or difficulty.

The document concludes with an appeal for scientific study of sex questions, with that sturdy realism that always characterises Quaker thought on these spiritual issues. However vague and indescribable the ends of human experience may seem, the first step in the right direction is always taken with a knowledge of fact. This generation has brought its feelings out into the light of day in a manner that would have shocked its grandparents; and that is to the good, as long as the new knowledge is to be used for its true end, the service of personality and the ripening of understanding to the knowledge of God.

Quakerism, by virtue of its close-knit community, has not had to face the problem of divorce in the way it presents itself, for example, to the Church of England, where the church has ceremonial responsibilities to those who are virtually non-members. Hitherto the problem has been much smaller, therefore, than the Anglican one, and it has been possible to treat failures in the same way as failures in any spiritual endeavour. The Society has therefore made no difficulty about the remarriage of its members (a notable contrast, incidentally, with the fuss it used to make when its members married non-members, and were expelled from the Society in their hundreds). There has been no compromise of the ideal of a lifelong union in the spirit, but it has not been felt necessary to bolster up the ideal by the external – and plainly ineffective – support of a veto on a new start when one has collapsed. This is not because Quakers have any special immunity from matrimonial difficulty; they have failed, as others have failed. But their answer is to turn in upon the source of light rather than to devise machinery for a defensive morality, and though machinery is sometimes necessary, it has not been felt that it has come to that yet. Perhaps the unhappy memory of the 'disownments' for 'marrying out' lingers to make them tolerant. But Friends believe they are right to put their faith whole heartedly in spiritual means to this subtle spiritual end.

If this profound, unquestioning respect for personality is the first element in a loving personal relationship, the second is simple honesty, 'plainness', as early Friends would have called it, integrity, clearness, the certainty that a man is indeed trafficking with another, and not the pretence of another. It is here that the Quaker testimony against formal oaths has its relevance. After a long struggle, members of the Society are now entitled to use a 'solemn affirmation' in a court of law, instead of invoking the name of God to make the assertion of *this* moment more solemn, more likely to be true, than the assertions of other moments. We cannot deal with others as persons, Friends have believed, unless we deal with them always in the truth; unless a chance encounter over a trivial matter is based as firmly – if not as widely – on reality as the most complex and significant relationship. Nor can we deal with our enemies as persons unless we speak the truth to them as we should to our friends. Therefore there can be no tacit admission, as is implied in the swearing of an oath, that there can be furtive moments when truth may be suppressed or distorted without harm. Men are easily misled by their passions and prejudices into the selection of facts to suit their own ends: we lie, not always because we want to, but because we have to. This knavery of our lower selves needs perpetual watchfulness, un-remitting attention to the claims of reality; and if we once acknowledge that in certain circumstances we are right to be specially watchful, we admit that there are other circumstances when we are 'right' to be unwatchful.

This is not fanciful, but a matter of plain commonsense. There are indeed times when telling the truth carries more weighty con-sequences than it does at other times, and the taking of evidence in a court of law is one of them. But if we are in the habit of picking our facts and shaping our interpretation of them to suit ourselves, then at the great moment we are incapable of facing facts squarely. The eye needs training in the reading of a micro-meter, and even more do our selfish emotions need training in keeping out of the way when facts are being observed. If in the trivialities of which the lives of even distinguished men are made we habitually persuade others and ourselves of what we want to believe, then in the critical turning points of our lives we shall be capable of nothing but a lie.

In this earnest attention to the importance of the trivial, Friends have won the reputation of a lack of proportion, of stiffness and obstinacy in refusing to change their minds, of being pernickety and 'difficult'. Such truth as there is in the charge – and there is certainly some – is due to the defect of high purpose. If the choice is presented between a triviality that lowers the meaning of life and an earnestness that raises it, we should all know where we stand. And if in the choice some people seem to lose a sense of humour, then those who keep it will have the more to exercise it on, and it is not only the non-Friend who sometimes finds himself forced to smile at a Quaker oddity. But some measure of oddity is inseparable from sincerity. We can look alike, and cause each other no amusement, if we dress alike, behave alike, and speak nothing but platitude; but if we did we should not be persons, and there could be no real relationship between us. We grow to love each other in the depths of our individuality, beneath the surface of conventionality and etiquette. And if to the outward

eye those depths are strange, they are none the less real, and
form the area of our deepest understanding.

Respect and integrity are the first two 'notes' in the harmony
of fellowship. But, it might be objected, there is nothing particularly Christian about these. They may, indeed, be described as
the flower of humanism – respect for human personality, respect
for truth, and there is nothing for Christian apologetic to deplore
in this admission. The specifically Christian element in them both
is their increased scope, the power to respect what may be rather
than what is, and the power to be truthful even when the truth is
apparently going to do one harm. And, indeed, even these lengths
may be reached by the spirit of humanism, leaving to Christian
love only the intangible difference of its powerful entwining with
the person of Christ, the tenderness of respect, and the humility
of truthfulness that spring from him.

But if this is true, of these things, it is not true of the third
element, which has indeed, in humanism, no name. St. Paul
called it charity. Modern writers have despaired of finding a word,
and have transliterated the Greek and written of *agape,* and left
it at that. It is the element which comes into the situation when
personal conflict becomes irreconcilable, and by all the rules must
lead to strife. It is possible to some extent to prevent a final conflict by the use of common sense, and this the Quaker will do as
long as he may. He will, in the words of a Yearly Meeting Epistle
of 1692:

> first speak privately to the party concerned, and endeavour reconciliation
> between themselves; and not to whisper or aggravate matters against
> others behind their backs, to the making of parties, and to the widening
> of the breach.

He will thus refrain, even then, from going to law, which has the
effect of declaring the breach open, and of preventing its closing
by more personal means.

He will also, if this fails, strive to

> maintain that charity which suffereth long and is kind. Put the best
> construction upon the conduct and opinions one of another which
> circumstances will warrant . . . Let each be tender of the reputation of
> his brother, and be earnest to possess the ornament of a meek and quiet
> spirit. Watch over one another for good but not for evil; and whilst not
> blind to the faults or false views of others, be especially careful not
> to make them a topic of common conversation. And in those cases in
> which it may be necessary to disclose the failings of others, be well

satisfied as to the purity of your own motives, before making them the subject of even confidential communication, whether verbally or by letter.°

All this is plain wisdom, to be advanced as counsel by anyone who has lived long enough and sensitively enough. But the test of Christian love comes when it has failed, when one side to the dispute has been patient and prudent, and has avoided provocation, and has acted in perfect integrity and is met by continuing hostility. The human reaction now is to extinguish the opponent's claim with all the force of law and the authority of reason and social order. The Christian reaction, argues the Quaker, is to accept the loss, or the shame or the suffering which the enemy is preparing in a last effort to touch the springs of personality.

> Christ died for us even when we were enemies, he has followed us by his Spirit in our many wanderings, he has borne with us in long-suffering pity; and if we hope to be forgiven, we must also forgive one another. He who yields to a suspicious and unforgiving spirit is led unto imagine things against his brother that are exaggerated, or even false. How can he, whose only hope is in the Lord's mercy, indulge in hard and unforgiving thoughts towards a brother or a sister ... Consider how exceeding broad is the new commandment of the Lord: 'Love one another, as I have loved you.' Wait not until thy brother be reconciled unto thee, or until he shall make the first overture. Be thyself the first to seek reconciliation, and to prove that thou art honestly desirous to submit thyself to the government of the Prince of Peace.°°

It is common to regard 'forgiveness' as an act which takes place when the dispute and the suffering is over. 'We have fought it out: let us forgive and be friends.' But in the Christian experience forgiveness never strays from its original meaning – 'to give intensely.' And through the whole course of a personal conflict, while all is done that prudence can suggest in the way of courtesy and the struggle towards understanding, in the avoidance of ill feeling and the irritation of gossip, there is still needed a steady process of giving, the creative effort to attain an understanding in the depths, to love at the heart of personality. And when, as will happen, the gift is spurned, the final fact in the situation is that Jesus died with his gift spurned, and was yet not only free from bitterness but full of love.

The story of early Quakerism is full of episodes in which this

°*Yearly Meeting Epistle*, 1834.
°°*Yearly Meeting Epistles*, 1870, 1872.

creative love bore its ultimate burden: tenderness towards gaolers, courageous patience with hooligans breaking up a meeting for worship and the like. And when the early zeal had died down, something of the same spirit remained, in the attitude to thieves and footpads ('Friend, what can have brought thee to this?' one Quaker is reputed to have said when he was held up on the road; and a Quakeress said to a man trying to snatch her purse, 'Let us kneel down on the pavement and ask Heavenly Father whether He means thee to have it.') and on until the latest opportunity for patience in the treatment awarded to conscientious objectors in the first, and to some extent in the second, world war. To the outward, unseeing eye this is a defeatist attitude: to the Christian it is the way he may best share in the experience of Christ.

And as the death of Christ was the means for the life of the church, so it has been found that loving to this ultimate point is creative and life-giving. To appeal to the community of humanity at its deepest is to create it at its deepest: to appeal to the fear and defensiveness on the surface is to leave the deepest life untouched. In the establishment of personal relations, 'he that seeketh his life shall lose it, and he that loseth his life for my sake shall find it.' For if, however courteously and legally, we live unto ourselves, we shall inevitably find that we live by ourselves. It is only as we are drawn in to the love of God for man, counting ourselves and our own concerns nothing beside the great joy and pain of it, that we find the unity with man that is our destiny.

CHAPTER ELEVEN

Creative Love: Economic Relationships

T HIS unity between one man and another, desperately difficult though it be to attain in reality, is not difficult to envisage as an ideal. Common human experience can be illuminated by the example and witness of Christ; and we can at least talk together of the love of man, and find each other talking the same language. The path is less clear when we begin to consider the relationship of groups of men, classes and nations, and the relationship between men in trade and commerce. It has always been clear to Friends that economic and political relation ships come under the judgement of God in precisely the same way as individual relationships. It is not enough to argue that business is business and politics is politics. All life is sacred, and is to be lived 'in the light'.

But while there is a certain simplicity in revolutionary relationships so long as they affect only oneself, the extension of them to a network of wider relationships introduces a baffling amount of complexity. To enter on a road that leads to suffering is easy enough so long as the suffering affects oneself alone: but as soon as it involves others, it presents a new challenge to thought, and a new urgency in the need to be sure of being right. In the development of its ethics, Quakerism has, as we have seen, followed a perfectionist principle, the belief that loving behaviour was to be evoked by behaving as if men were already loving, and accepting the consequences if the act of faith failed. This was possible in private relations between individuals, but when it was applied to economic or political relations it meant one of two things. The Quaker could either withdraw from the situation altogether, and keep his hands free of evil as a testimony; or he could make some sort of compromise with evil, and while working in a corrupt system, seek to raise the general level of behaviour by education and persuasion.

In the course of events, Quakers chose both: perfectionism in politics and compromise in business. In the one they erected the pacifist principle to the nearest thing to a dogma they have ever possessed; in the other, they went into business with their eyes open for opportunities to do good within the limits imposed by the economic order, but with oddly little insight into the vices of that order itself. Modern Friends would point to the peace testimony as the most significant piece of Quaker witness, because of its consistency and clarity; but it is arguable that the compromises of the economic life of Friends will in the long run be seen to be more valuable.

They have at least been more effective, for Quakers have exerted an influence on economic affairs beyond all proportion to their numbers, while their influence on international affairs has so far been negligible. They would argue that this is merely because it is before its time, and the day will come when its 'rightness' will be seen and its immediate relevance accepted. Until then, the clear, unmistakable perfectionism is the best they can do. And while this may be true in that context, it is certainly true that in this other context compromise has permitted certain achievement which perfectionism would have prevented. The compromise has brought its own problems, which in this time of general anxiety and lack of direction distress the Society to the point of bewilderment, but bewilderment in one generation is not necessarily the result of error by another: it may be caused merely by lack of insight on its own part. And it is conceivable that had the dedication and vision and power of the early Friends survived throughout the whole three hundred years of Quaker history, the contrast between divided aims in industrial organization and clear aims in international organization would never have arisen. For early Friends had no thought that they were compromising when they took up the world's business, and they were ready to take on political responsibility just as eagerly. Where one Friend set up a factory, another set up Pennsylvania. And it is possible that if there had been enough *life* for it all, there might have been more economic idealism and more political realism, to produce a genuine 'social gospel'.

Be that as it may, the story of Quakers in industrial affairs, vexing though it is to the more radical members of the Society, is not without interest, and in two ways they made contributions which were of value in themselves, and were distinctive of the Quaker position at large.

In the first place they brought into business relationships the same quality of loving interdependence that they had already brought into personal relationships. It was not, perhaps, the full, sacrificial love of the Cross, but respect for personality and personal integrity were present in liberal measure. Quakers were always conscious that servants and employees were so only by reason of function and not because of any personal inferiority. Their domestic servants were often to be found performing the evangelistic work of the Society alongside their masters. Educational and co-operative measures were frequently taken in Quaker factories. And integrity, honesty and plain dealing, even though we all pay lip-service to it in these days when the omnipresence of auditors makes it difficult not to, was rare enough in the seventeenth century to demand deep spiritual insight.

Quakers set up their standards because they knew them to be right, and with no vision beyond; and it was almost embarrassing to find that honesty was the best business policy after all. Fox comments on it:

> At the first convincement, when Friends could not put off their hats to people, or say You to a single person, but Thou and Thee; when they could not bow, or use flattering words in salutations, or adopt the fashions and customs of the world, many Friends, that were tradesmen of several sorts, lost their custom at the first; for the people were shy of them, and would not trade with them; so that for a time some Friends could hardly get money enough to buy bread. But afterwards, when people came to have experience of Friends' honesty and truthfulness, and found that their Yea was yea, and the Nay was nay; that they kept to a word in their dealings, and that they would not cozen and cheat them; but that if they sent a child to their shops for anything, they were as well used as if they had come themselves; the lives and conversations of Friends did preach, and reached to the witness of God in the people. Then things altered so, that all the inquiry was, 'Where is there a draper, or shopkeeper, or tailor, or shoemaker, or any other tradesman, that is a Quaker?' Insomuch that Friends had more trade than many of their neighbours, and if there was any trading, they had a great part of it. Then the envious professors altered their note, and began to cry out, 'If we let these Quakers alone, they will take the trade of the nation out of our hands.'*

John Woolman dealt with this situation for himself by giving up several 'lines' that he had formerly sold in his shop, by way of reducing his care and leaving himself free for the real business of life. And before this, he had chosen a humble calling rather than a great one:

*Journal.

I had several offers of business that appeared profitable, but saw not my way clear to accept of them, as believing the business proposed would be attended with more outward care and cumber than was required of me to engage in. I saw that a humble man, with the blessing of the Lord, might live on little; and that where the heart was set on greatness success in business did not satisfy the craving; but that commonly with an increase of wealth, the desire for wealth increased.°

But though the results of honest dealing were – and still are – embarrassing to men who believe that simplicity is an essential part of their ordering of their lives, there is nothing wrong with honest dealing in itself, and the abolition of haggling and the establishment of the fixed price was an improvement in economic machinery to which Friends made a considerable contribution. That the testimony was dependent on the whole spiritual position of Friends, and was used to spread the light, may be seen from these words of an early pamphleteer, writing to Friends:

Do not be drawn forth into many words in answering those who are not in the dread and fear of the Lord. After you have put a price on your commodities which is equal, and you can sell them; then if the persons you are dealing with multiply words, stand you silent in the fear, dread and awe of God, and this will answer the witness of God in them you are dealing with.°°

Other aspects of the same plainness and honesty were an emphasis on the strict keeping of accounts – an emphasis continued to this day in Advices and Queries; punctilious fulfilment of contracts and engagements; reminders to members of the Christian courtesy implicit in making one's will:

Knowing the uncertainty of life, it is strongly recommended that Friends make their wills in time of health and strength of judgement, to prevent the inconvenience, loss and trouble that may fall upon their relatives and friends through their dying intestate. We counsel that none postpone this duty to a sick bed, an improper time to settle our outward affairs. Even if we should be favoured with a clear understanding, this ought not to be diverted from a grave consideration of the approaching solemn change. Making his will in due time can shorten no man's days, but omission and delay have proved very injurious to many.°°°

This counsel is continued into the very principles that should guide the dispositions themselves, and such practical reminders as the fact that marriage revokes a will already made.

°John Woolman: *Journal.*
°°Charles Marshall: *Epistle to the Flock of Jesus Christ.*
°°°*Christian Practice.*

All this prudent conscientiousness in business was a source of profit to Friends, and however pure the original motives, there is a certain lack of spiritual challenge in behaviour that may be seen to be highly profitable. We have cause to be grateful to the early Friends who thus increased the justice and equity of economic relations; but though we have cause, it is the way of things that we should be less grateful than we might have been if they had made their improvements without benefiting themselves. And though we recognize their integrity, we look in vain for the third element, the sacrificial giving that is the distinctive mark of Christian love. They gave, these early Friends: they gave to their own workmen, to the poor, to the Society and to its work. And to the present day, when private fortunes are in any case drying up, many pieces of costly and valuable Christian work have been rendered possible, and sustained through difficult times, by substantial benefactions. But to give from a fortune can never be the same thing as casting the mite into the treasury; and it has become an increasing preoccupation with Friends, this missing dimension in economic affairs.

Something of the same deficiency marks the other great contribution that Friends have made, in the great increase in technical proficiency for which they are responsible. It was inevitable that if Friends went into business, they would be more than competent at it, for the best brains of the Society were compelled to enter trade rather than anything else. Like other Dissenters, they were excluded from the universities, and therefore from the professions, except from medicine, for which special arrangements were possible at Edinburgh. They were excluded from politics for the same reason, and also because, after the 'holy experiment' in Pennsylvania, the perfectionist tendency set a barrier to their progress. So into business they went, with not only, like other Dissenters, the whole of their intellectual competence untapped by other occupations, but with a special quality of flexibility, open mindedness, and readiness to innovate, which was to prove singularly apt in the industrial revolution already inevitable but not yet foreseen. The detailed story of their innovations may be read in the study of *Quakers in Science and Industry* by Arthur Raistrick. For our purpose it is enough to recall the names of Barclay and Lloyd, or the Darbys of Coalbrookdale, as examples of men whose insight into the conditions of their task enabled them to change the whole direction of it.

10

It is the old note of insight again. The Inward Light is not limited to the production of a peculiar kind of unworldliness: it is the whole interpretation of life itself. And a community who develop the habit of asking the meaning of all they see, as part of their quest for God, cannot lay the habit aside when they face a technical problem. As scientific realism is an element in the Quaker curriculum of education, so it is in their attitude to life.

But this further distinctively Quaker contribution to economic life is still unsatisfactory. Integrity and ingenuity – are these an adequate harvest of the Seed of the blood of Christ? If a ship were to be sailed into the jaws of hell, it would be no reasonable grounds of salvation to have been honest and punctilious in cleaning the decks, or to have invented a gadget that cleaned them more efficiently. And under the judgement of the radical criticism of this generation, there has arisen a feeling that Quakerism has been busy cleaning the decks and inventing devices – and being handsomely rewarded for its faithfulness – but has not seen the whirlpool towards which the ship of state is being steered. The failure, if failure there be, is one of understanding rather than attitude. Friends have been looking in the right direction, even though they may not have seen far enough. As early as the seventeenth century there was sign of an awareness of the meaning of poverty, and a concern for the poor 'in the large' as well as individually, which might have made the basis of a radical social criticism. Bellers, for example, in his *Proposals for Raising a College of Industry* (1696) writes:

> I often having thought of the misery of the poor of this nation, and at the same time have reckoned them the treasure of it, the labour of the poor being the mines of the rich, and beyond all that Spain is master of; and many thoughts have run through me how then it comes that the poor should be such a burden, and so miserable, and how it might be prevented; whilst I think it as much more charity to put the poor in a way to live by honest labour, than to maintain them idle, as it would be to set a man's broken leg, that he might go himself, rather than always to carry him.

Bellers carried his thought out in a wide sweep, embracing juvenile delinquency, penal reform, health insurance, and electoral reform – and this before the industrial revolution had done its worst.

But the Society as a whole somehow missed the sense of urgency and long-sightedness that characterised Bellers, and turned to the quiet faithfulness and ingenuity that seemed their obvious duty.

Another hopeful moment in the next century was the abolition of slavery, which was precisely the kind of controversial issue, striking down to the depths of the belief about man, that might perhaps have set off a whole train of radical re-examination of the social order. Quakers were well to the fore in the struggle against slavery itself, but they failed to carry their position through to the end. The nineteenth century saw an effort, sponsored by John Bright, to carry the Quaker insight into politics, but this was in any case doomed to failure. There can be no politics of the Cross until the people have all embraced the way of the Cross for themselves; and a cabinet cannot be more Christian than the nation.

And so the action of the Society continued to be tactical and palliative rather than strategic and radical. This was not characteristic of Quaker testimony in other fields. The typical method was absolutism, perfectionism, at whatever cost, even to death, leaving the world to come to terms with Quaker ideals rather than bringing the ideals into line with the world. It can be argued that in this matter a larger measure of compromise is necessary than in some others. Without living for a time, at least, one cannot even die a martyr's death. Even Jesus had his thirty years. And if one is to live for a time, one cannot be completely purist about the ultimate source of income: a shopkeeper sells to knaves, and makes his profit out of their knavery. And despite the perfectionist trait, there has always been a sturdy determination among Friends to live by an incarnationist belief, and to express their spiritual ideals in the places where men live and congregate. William Penn was quite clear in his own mind that Quakers must work alongside others, and live their love in co-operation rather than challenge:

> True godliness does not turn men out of the world, but enables them to live better in it, and excites their endeavours to mend it. Christians should keep the helm and guide the vessel to its port, not meanly steal out at the stern of the world, and leave those that are in it without a pilot, to be driven by the fury of evil times upon the rock or sand of ruin.°

When once the decision has been taken to accept the general conditions of the industrial system, the Quaker emphasis on the establishment of good personal relations within it is both valuable and necessary. At one time they were the only group of employers

°*No Cross, No Crown.*

in the field with an appreciation of what it meant. Today they are no longer alone, but they are still needed. There are still industries – and some of them socially owned – where the plain commonsense of loving relationships is not even dimly understood: where management and labour are two separate forces, vaguely hostile, acutely suspicious, barely understanding each other. The planning of human relationships *within* the present system is still desperately necessary; and may, indeed, have to be realized in some measure *before* radical reconstruction of the whole system is possible. It is difficult to make an economic peace treaty while the forces on both sides are still fighting; and some measure of experiment in small groups may be required before there can be any real conception of what harmony means in a whole economic order.

The embarrassing feature of the Quaker method has always been its success. Faithfulness to spiritual law ought not, we feel, to lead to material profit. But the central element in the whole Quaker position is that spiritual laws are material laws too: they are the laws of the universe. This has come to be recognized in modern medicine, where there is a steadily increasing tendency to look for the causes of physical illness in disorders of the personality; and it is possible to claim the same relationship in economic affairs. 'Seek ye first the kingdom of heaven, and all these things shall be added unto you.' And there is no call to be embarrassed when Jesus is found to have been right, and 'these things' are added in abundance. The important word in the statement is 'first'. We cannot seek the kingdom of God as a means to the securing of 'all these things', any more than we can successfully pursue mental health as a means to physical health. We pursue the higher goods for their own sake, and the lower good follows. But if we try to seek the higher for the sake of the lower, the system breaks down. It is the ultimate exploitation, the cultivation of good human relations because they 'pay' well.

The danger is that they do 'pay' well, as Quaker and other good employers have shown; but the modern discussion of human relations in industry, which has become fashionable since the war, is largely based on the desire to correct this element in the whole industrial situation in the interests of greater productivity. Works canteens, welfare officers, 'music while you work' and the five-day week are all justified on these grounds. And they may, indeed, lead to a certain improvement in the situation – they will in so far as they are good in themselves – but in the end, 'all these things' depend on viewing human relations, not as a technical device for the improvement of the machine, but as the end towards which the machine is devised. Managers and employees must matter to each other as persons if they are to serve to the full the ends for which they have banded themselves together. And in the emphasis on this truth, as necessary now as ever, the Quaker tradition of industrial organization has still a vital part to play.

Indeed the embarrassing thing about successful industry is not the wealth it produces, but the fact that we have not yet devised a system of just division of the wealth. The rewards are not too great, but they are too great for some and too little for others; and Quaker business men have been no more far-sighted than anyone else in seeing how to solve this problem. They have not, furthermore – and this is really the more important – found a way of associating their workpeople in the control of the business in anything more than a tentative way. The word 'employee' is still applicable to Quaker organisation, and it fails to chime with the word 'friend'. These two problems, of control and reward, have not yet been solved by industry at large, and there is no blame to be attached to Friends for being baffled by them, but it must be admitted that there is as yet little characteristically Quaker contribution being made to their solution.

There are signs that a more radical type of thought is beginning to arise, and Friends have committed themselves to certain general principles which are none the less relevant for being slightly vague. They may be seen in this statement of the foundations of a true social order, adopted by Yearly Meeting in 1918.

The Fatherhood of God, as revealed by Jesus Christ, should lead us towards a Brotherhood which knows no restriction of race, sex or social class.

This Brotherhood should express itself in a social order which is directed, beyond all material ends, to the growth of personality truly related to God and man.

The opportunity of full development, physical, moral and spiritual, should be assured to every member of the community, man, woman, and child. The development of man's full personality should not be hampered by unjust conditions nor crushed by economic pressure.

We should seek a way of living that will free us from the bondage of material things and mere conventions, that will raise no barrier between man and man, and will put no excessive burden of labour upon any by reason of our superfluous demands.

The spiritual force of righteousness, loving-kindness and trust is mighty, because of the appeal it makes to the best in every man, and when applied to industrial relations, achieves great things.

Our rejection of the methods of outward domination, and of the appeal to force, applies not only to international affairs, but to the whole problem of industrial control. Not through antagonism but through co-operation and goodwill can the best be attained for each and all.

Mutual service should be the principle upon which life is organized. Service, not private gain, should be the motive of all work.

The ownership of material things, such as land and capital, should be so regulated as best to minister to the need and development of man.°

This is all unexceptionable, as far as it goes, but phrases such as 'regulated . . . . to minister to . . . . the development of man' would be agreed on by all parties to our present social order without calling for any sacrifice from anyone. Some progress was made in the period between the wars, when the extent of unemployment called out the best of the Quaker effort. Here was a concrete situation, like a famine or a bombed town, into which they could go with dedication, clear purpose, and the gift of human understanding. In consequence recreation centres, aid with food and goods, settlements, camps and other schemes came into being; and Quaker initiative stirred numerous other agencies and individuals to similar effort. About the same time a standing committee was set up to study the underlying problems – the Industrial and Social Order Council – which has continued to this day to represent the economic thought of the Society. It has not entirely convinced the Society as a whole, but it survives and stirs the Quaker conscience, without yet being in a position to offer a clear call to action.

The difficulty does not lie solely in the inertia of a society traditionally successful in the industrial system (though success is a powerful disincentive to radical criticism of the conditions of success). It lies even more in the fact that the radical solutions so far offered for our choice seem to be to some extent in conflict with traditional Quaker concepts. How is the control of industry to be rendered 'democratic'? The doctrine of the inner light implies that all men need to have a measure of choice and independence in their work: if God is to speak to us only of our leisure, our religion does not reach far. Man thus needs the opportunity to make decisions, to choose, to bring responsible thought to bear upon his work. In a co-operative civilization he will not be free, of course, to do 'just what he likes'. But then, as

°*Christian Practice*

we have seen, Quakers, for all their individualism, have always found a way of dealing with people who do 'just as they like'; and it would be easy to extend the principles of Quaker business machinery into the world's business.

What is not so easy is to see how to devise the opposite process: not to control the individualist, but to enlist his aid. The evils of large-scale capitalist monopoly are plain; but to the Quaker, seeking to bend industrial organization to 'the growth of personality truly related to God and man', a socialist monopoly, however correctly controlled, seems to offer little cause for rejoicing. It would be better to travel in a comfortable, well-ordered liner than in a pirate ship; but if they are both going the wrong way it would be as well to stay at home; and Quakerism regards all large industrial units as wrongly directed.

But the small, 'family' business, in which owner and workpeople can indeed be 'friends', and can together devise a system of joint ownership and control, is no longer adequate. There are some tasks it can still fulfill, but it cannot run a railway or an air line or a post office. Where it is still relevant, the Quaker has something to say on how to run a family business; but though Quakers held much of the initiative in the development of the first railways, they have little to say nowadays about how to fit small units into the larger whole which we have forced on ourselves.

Similarly, there is no characteristic and original Quaker testimony on the subject of wages and rewards. Woolman's withdrawal from business because he found it too profitable has not been emulated. There has been a certain restraint on the profits themselves, and a vast amount of ploughing profits back into the firm on either its technical or personal side. But Quaker thought has accepted rather than initiated the vast process of social change which is leading to the disappearance of the private fortune. They have accepted it with relief, not only because it frees them of their historic embarrassment, but because they have always known that rewards must be secondary to the work itself. When wages vary enormously, it is futile to preach the sanctity of labour; but in a society beginning to approach economic equality there is need to speak of the joy of work seen as service, not only to the community, but to the Creator of the community. The early insistence on a just price was only an aspect of this belief. Price, and wages, are not to be fixed by the indifferent operation of laws of supply and demand, any more than by the varying cunning and ruthlessness of the parties. The demand must operate to control the *supply*, but not to control the price of what is supplied. It never has done entirely, of course: off-season eggs, however rare, have never risen to the price of new motor-cars, however common; and prices must always follow to some extent, and ideally more and more closely, the value of the work done, in terms of the needs of those who do it.

But the sanctity of labour means more than this, for it means that men should come to see in the very work itself something that is of value because it is part of the whole attitude to life which gives the universe its value. Work can never for all people be done 'for the fun of it', nor 'for the love of it' if by love is meant liking, pleasure, delight. But all men can work for the love of God, and take their 'reward' not as reward at all, but as the means to a life that is full of love and service and joy in work and play.

Friends may thus be seen to have applied the essential principle of their testimony to the industrial order, and to have a general concept of the goal of their effort, without any clear idea of how they are to reach it. They have, indeed, been too practical a body in the past to be able to take the lead in an age of planning; and they would approach with some justifiable suspicion an attempt to force their own judgement – however grandly it might be disguised as a 'plan' – upon other men who are not allowed the opportunity to use their own insight. As they would reject the revolutionary method of securing justice for the working man, so they would shrink from the imposition on society of a complex organization devised by a few. They are by belief and tradition likely to be bad planners.

But a significant change has taken place in the Society in the last generation which may have a bearing on this problem. The universities have been open to Dissenters for a hundred years, and Quakers have thus been freed from the pressure to enter business. They have taken advantage of their opportunity so fully that the membership of the Society is now very largely professional – teaching, research, the social sciences. From a combination of this new outlook and intellectual equipment and the old empirical attitude there may emerge a social criticism that will preserve the spiritual realities by which the Society has lived, and yet solve the technical problems which Quaker business has inevitably found too much for it.

Radical criticism – and this must be remembered when we feel impatient with Quaker testimony in the past – is not enough. Someone, somewhere, must bring it to bear upon the realities of the situation. Someone must live it. It is not enough to produce a scheme whereby human beings can love each other efficiently: someone must start the loving. And it is there that the Quaker genius may show itself. In 1925 Yearly Meeting expressed just this hope, calling for the creation of a social order in which 'every able adult citizen should be a producer in the widest sense of the term and free to take an effective share in directing his own labour', and in which 'possession of property would no longer confer rights of control over the lives of others', but 'resources would be socially organized for common advantage', – the old, vague generalities again – and then speaking with surely a greater warmth, an awakening note of dedication:

> We have not lived sufficiently in the spirit of love, brotherhood, meekness, and gentleness, nor sought to bring these gifts to bear on the fabric of life. We have been too ready to take things as we found them, and have not tried sufficiently to mould all according to the teaching and life of our divine Master.
>
> If we are rightly to readjust our own lives and effectually to help those of others, we must needs experience the impelling power of a divine love for mankind.
>
> Our attitude towards life should tend to free us from the bondage of material things, and make us concerned to give the first place to the things of the spirit. The main purpose of the existence of the Church is to work for the coming of that Kingdom of Heaven on earth, for which Jesus Christ lived and died. It is as we all devote ourselves to working for a new spirit in the relations of men, and for a new social order more in accordance with the mind of Christ, that we shall recognise how much the possession of wealth and of the power derived from wealth may blunt the sense of social justice in the owners, and hinder their opportunities for spiritual work, and that we shall come to recognize as superfluous things which perhaps we formely regarded as necessaries. So shall we be ready to examine without prejudice new proposals toward better social relationships. Let us believe in the possibility of reconstruction and seek actively for new light. Let us make experiments, and pray that out of this period of strife and change a new and better order may arise. Let us show ourselves a community which believes in the practicability of the Kingdom of God.°

Here at last is the authentic Quaker note—'a community which believes in the practicability of the Kingdom of God'. The witness of the Society has been rendered hesitant because it
°*Christian Practice.*

CHAPTER TWELVE

Creative Love: International Relationships

THE clearest and most celebrated Quaker testimony is the refusal to carry arms. On this issue both members and non-members know where the Society of Friends stands, far more clearly than on any other ethical issue. In one sense, therefore, it is the simplest testimony to state, involving as it does a clear line of action which may be followed in all circumstances. But in another sense, it is the most difficult of all Quaker testimonies to discuss, for its apparent simplicity is deceptive. Looked at from outside, as an action only, it seems merely negative, self-centred, unrealistic, irrelevant to the needs of the age; and if it is to be understood as it is intended it needs to be viewed from within in terms of intention and purpose.

One danger is that the clarity of it, and the virtual unanimity of the Society in following it, make it appear in the light of a 'party line', a mark of difference, a badge to keep the group together. This it is certainly not. On this issue, no more than on any other, is there an authoritative ruling, binding on the members. The fact that the Society *is* almost completely agreed means that the issue has to be taken seriously by young Friends growing up, to a greater extent than would be normal in another denomination; and the fact that parents and older friends have suffered for their pacifism means that young Friends are faced by a strong challenge which they cannot easily ignore; but this is no party line.

The other danger is that a testimony which appeared inevitable in the seventeenth century may be accepted in the twentieth, both by members and non-members, as a Quaker peculiarity, without seeing its implications in the new situation. It was one thing to refuse to wear or use a sword. Is it the same thing to stand idle while two halves of the world begin to rain bombs on each other?

The original stand was, granted the general Quaker position, inevitable. The sects were at war, seeking to determine the will of God for the church by seeing which group of men could establish its physical and political supremacy. Fox and his followers perceived, what most of us would now agree, that the one was not settled by the other. Even then it was recognized that trial by combat did not settle who was right in a dispute between individuals. It had not then been recognized that it was equally irrelevant to attempt to settle by combat who was right in a dispute between two groups. It was seriously believed that God would be a party to the struggle, and would strengthen the arms of the side he wished to win. This Friends denied. 'If my kingdom were of this world, then would my children fight.' But it was not of this world. It was a spiritual kingdom, built of love and faith and truth and tenderness; and these were the first victims of war. The kingdom could not come by a method that started by destroying it.

And if war were thus condemned by orthodox Christian doctrine, as Friends understood it, the condemnation was increased by the peculiar Quaker emphasis on the light within. If the most important fact about a human being was his capacity for the knowledge of God, then conflicts, as well as agreements, must be based on that principle. Killing a man meant that he could no longer live a Christian life: it was to put an end to his power of seeing God in this life, whatever it might mean for the life beyond (and unrealistic though Friends have been accused of being, they have never let speculation about an entirely unknown other life overrule the plain facts of this one). To kill a man is to deny that he has any right to live, and that is to deny that God has any interest in him. But that is to deny the whole creative purpose of God:

> Now the Lord God hath opened to me by his invisible power how that every man was enlightened by the divine Light of Christ; and I saw it shine through all.[*]

Some might deny the light, but they were in it. It shone through them. It was what they were there for. And to kill them because they were in error was to give up hope of them, to assert that the light had now no more part in them, and they were wholly dark. But God did not give us up because we were in error, but unchangeably 'shone through us'.

War, indeed, the Quaker diagnosis continued, was the evil in

[*]Fox: *Journal.*

us seeking to triumph. Even if we chose a relatively righteous cause, it was evil, the desire for power and domination, that made us fight for it. Wars arose 'even from the lust'. For if we lose the desire for power and domination (and if we learn to desire what Christ desired we cannot but lose it) then there is nothing to fight for. This is the source of the Quaker certainty that war is in all circumstances wrong. Certain moral principles may find varying expression in varying circumstances – as a parent may love by granting one day and love by refusing another – but if war springs from the lust for power it is always wrong.

Christian Practice significantly prints a succession of statements, issued during war after war, reiterating the same position. The War of the Austrian Succession prompted Yearly Meeting in 1744 to remind Friends of their witness

> against bearing arms and fighting, that by a conduct agreeable to our profession we may demonstrate ourselves to be real followers of the Messiah, the peaceable Saviour, of the increase of whose government and peace there shall be no end.

In 1805, when the nation was in the mood of despondence that preceded the triumph of Trafalgar, Yearly Meeting called upon them to

> guard against placing your dependence on fleets and armies.

During the Crimean War they repeated their affirmation:

> We feel bound explicitly to avow our continued unshaken persuasion that all war is utterly incompatible with the plain precepts of our Divine Lord and Lawgiver, and with the whole spirit and tenor of His Gospel; and that no plea of necessity or of policy, however urgent or peculiar, can avail to release either individuals or nations from the paramount allegiance which they owe unto him who hath said, 'Love your enemies'.

During the Boer War, a statement recalled the essential Quaker method of behaving as if the Kingdom of God were indeed at hand, as a means of bringing it in:

> It has been well said, 'It seems to be the will of Him who is infinite in wisdom, that light upon great subjects should first arise and be gradually spread through the faithfulness of individuals in acting up to their own convictions'. This was the secret of the power of the early church. The blood of the Christians proved a fruitful seed .. We covet a like faithful witness against war from Christians today.

And at last, when the conditions of war had changed unrecogniz-
ably, and pacifism became an issue for the Church at large, but
was felt in these conditions to be a mere abdication of responsibility, this statement was issued, in 1915:

> It is not enough to be satisfied with a barren negative witness, a mere
> proclamation of non-resistance. We must search for a positive vital con-
> structive message. Such a message, a message of supreme love, we find
> in the life and death of our Lord Jesus Christ. We find it in the doctrine
> of the indwelling Christ, that re-discovery of early Friends, leading as
> it does to a recognition of the brotherhood of all men. Of this doctrine
> our testimony as to war and peace is a necessary outcome, and if we
> understand the doctrine aright, and follow it in its wide implications, we
> shall find that it calls to the peaceable spirit and the rule of love in all
> the broad and manifold relations of life.

This burning clarity of conviction continued into the age of
total war, and it continues still. But it is one thing to be convinced
that your own action – or refusal of action – is right and relevant,
and another to convince the world; and total war has raised
a sharp challenge to Quaker pacifism. It was legitimate to refuse
to fight for a party within the state, at a time when an individual
was under no necessity to join a party at all. It was legitimate
to refuse to fight for the state at a time when an individual
was under no compulsion to fight at all. But how now, when
not only is there conscription – the means by which the state
makes provision for its own survival – but also war waged by
means, and to an extent, that involve everybody, whether they
like it or not? If a pacifist stays in England during a war, he must
live on food that has been brought in convoy, not only defended
by naval guns, but bought with the blood of men who long for
peace to the extent of giving their lives for it, many of them
sincere Christians who have learnt from their Master to hate
violence and bloodshed and yet have chosen deliberately what to
them is the harder way, because they feel it their duty. No longer
is the soldiery 'brutal and licentious', the group-representation of
the lust for power: the soldiery is the people, loving peace, and
reluctantly performing nauseous deeds to defend it.

And furthermore, when two powers mobilize all their forces in
a death struggle, the weakening of one by the withdrawal of even
a handful of people is a serious matter, which no sensitive person
can lightly agree to. If because of a streak of pacifist conviction,
one side enters the struggle lame and halting, and is defeated,
and suffers the consequences, is not the suffering to be laid to

the door of the pacifist? Can Christian love mean this? I have argued above that the Christian is aware of the doubts about his faith, and holds to his belief with his eyes open; and in the same way it is not to be believed that Friends are unaware of the force, not only of the argument on the other side, but of the depth and power of the worthy feelings from which they spring. Friends are not born without a love of their country, nor without sympathy with those they work with and live among. Nor are they without discrimination of the moral values involved in a struggle such as that between the Western powers and the strange evil that possessed the rulers of Germany in the darkest days. But if they were to find themselves living among angels and archangels, and war were to break out against the forces of hell, they would still be held in the compulsion of their faith. 'The Spirit of Christ . . . . will never move us to fight a war against any man with outward weapons, *neither for the kingdom of Christ* nor for the kingdoms of this world.' For when Christ himself, the very life of the Kingdom on earth, was assaulted by the powers of evil, he did not fight, but suffered and died.

Why are they so certain, even today, and even against the force of patriotism, contempt, the loss of personal friendship, and the appalling knowledge that but for the warring of these men whose claim on them they reject they might be dead themselves? What is the 'positive vital constructive message' that they rightly insist must be the burden of their apparently negative and highly dangerous line of action?

The central foundation of it lies in the belief that human power, however highly organized, however ruthless, is ultimately powerless against the spirit of God at work in man. 'Power' is the ability to compel the bodies of men to go through certain motions, to be carried about, to suffer pain, and to be extinguished, but though all this be done, there remains an aspect of personality which cannot be touched. It is this aspect which represents the significant part of man, the purpose of his life. And whatever may be done to his body, man remains in possession of a certain ultimate freedom of choice, of allying himself with truth, of 'standing' for something, even unto death. This freedom is man's opportunity to count for something, and to make his personal contribution to the life of the race, and however he may be forced to suffer, to have things done to him, it is here in his private freedom that man lives his real life. 'That which cometh out of the man, that defileth the man.'* Our most fruitful opportunity of making a distinctive contribution, therefore, is offered by those moments of frustration when the exercise of our freedom is most difficult, most costly. When we are free in body as well as in this inmost liberty of the will, we cannot show as clearly what we are made of as when we are faced by an apparently overwhelming challenge, as a sprinter cannot show what *he* is made of when he is driving a car. This is true of all our powers, but it is most relevant to the power of love. Loving our friends is easy. Loving our enemies is hard. But loving our enemies shows more of the meaning of love than loving our friends. The lesson goes deeper, and works on a profounder level.

The way to set love working in a loveless world is therefore to seek out the points of conflict and hate, and love in them instead of hating in them. If an enemy attacks, out of lust, or hate, or fear for himself, and he is met by lust and hate and fear in return, the struggle must grow more and more bitter until there is exhaustion. But if he is met by love and the serene confidence that he cannot touch the secret of life, there is a possibility that he will be 'found' by the new standard, and will respond with a dawning understanding of a new rôle for himself. I use the word 'possibility' deliberately. We have no evidence to suggest that in any situation perfect love will certainly drive out all hate. The crucifixion did not do it, and the martyrs of the Church did not do it. But if it were more than a possibility, if it were a certainty that love would always 'work', then love would be mere prudence, and Christianity would be obvious policy, paying better dividends than any other. God did not make the world like that, and though there have always been some to regret that he did not, if he had done, it would not have been the same world. If we are to be free to love, we must be free to hate; if free to obey, then free to disobey; if free to respond to love, then free not to respond. And though we may love our enemies, they are still free not to love us.

But if we believe that man is made for love, then we must believe that the highest hope is to love him. If he is true to his own nature, he will respond. If not, then we have failed, as others have failed before us. But the failure is still only failure, and the truth about man remains that he finds his destiny in love. If we lower our hope, we in effect change our belief, coming to the conclusion than man is not meant for love at all, but is meant

*Mark 7, 20.

to defend his own life and goods, and live unto himself.

In political terms, this means that a Christian pacifist state would refuse to defend itself when attacked. It might succeed at once, and the enemy might be awakened by the appeal to 'that of God' in their natures. This is the naive hope, and it has occasionally happened that warriors have refused to attack unarmed, unresisting men. But if it does not succeed – and it is only when it does not succeed that the Cross begins to bear its dreadful relevance – then the Christian nation begins to suffer, and to accept its suffering as an opportunity of letting into human life the triumphant love of God. If they were all to be butchered, and were to hold on to the last to the loving spirit of Christ on the cross, they would, one by one, have released the precious power they had been entrusted with, and have set it free to work upon the lust and hate that can be conquered in no other way.

But they would be dead, it will be argued. So was Jesus, and yet Christianity rose out of his death. So, incidentally, are the millions of men who have fought the worlds wars: but because they died under the command of a nation's desire to kill, their sacrifice has meant nothing in the world's journey towards love. It is the freely accepted death, the love freely offered and spent, that 'works'. The disciples could not conceive what was to happen to the world because Jesus was faithful; and we cannot conceive what would happen if a whole nation were to march to Calvary.

This is the ultimate picture of what the Christian pacifist is prepared to accept, because he believes that is the way the world was made. When we say that God is like Christ, we mean that the creation was planned for this, and that human life, for all its precious joy, finds its fulfilment in being given away. And when Jesus reminded his followers that they must take up their cross he meant, not that they should fill their lives with burdens, but that they should hold everything in readiness to be squandered if it were needed.

This stark, simple picture lies, as I have said, behind the pacifist position, and enters into the worship and prayer that lie at the centre of the Christian experience. But there has never been a wholly Christian nation, dedicated to the last man to this ultimate step. The kingdom of God has no territory of its own to be defended by this creative defencelessness. The position of the Christian pacifist is therefore complicated by his responsibilities to those who help to sustain his life, but who do not subscribe to his belief or his hope. He is not, in modern war, called upon to make his final sacrifice: indeed, he would be prevented from doing it, if he were to attempt it. It is here that the tension of the pacifist witness occurs, and it seems to many that pacifism becomes merely negative and irrelevant.

But Friends, though accepting the limitations of hard fact, have been unable to compromise on the central issue of bearing arms, and have sought instead to realize the concept of a community of love and understanding, stretching across the frontiers, to create slowly a living body of witness, across the lines of conflict, to the Christian judgement on the basic assumptions of warring states. The hope here is that the peoples on both sides of the conflict may come to recognize the immorality of war because a handful of their own members are taking their absolute stand outside it. The peaceful solution of a dispute is more sensible than an attempt to solve it by war because it is in harmony with the laws of the universe – in precisely the same way as it is more sensible to climb down a cliff than to jump off the top, because *that* is in harmony with the laws of the universe. And when whole peoples have developed the habit of jumping off the top to their destruction, there is surely something positive in the testimony of a few who climb down, and demonstrate the better way.

There is thus a place in the process of the political education of the race for a few who stand out, even at great cost to themselves, and press upon the attention of the rest the basic assumptions of their stand. There is need for utter clarity in this setting out of motive, as was demonstrated when pacifists and profiteers alike were bemused by the Munich policy of appeasement. Buying a postponement of war by tossing to the enemy a few titbits (particularly when the titbits belong to other nations) is no more positive than delaying the leap of an angry lion by tossing him a few mutton chops stolen from someone else's table. But to approach human beings, even angry human beings, in the courage that comes from complete dependence on the will of God, and to demonstrate that even here, in our anger and imperfection, we can begin the practice of loving obedience to spiritual law; to press this on both sides, and to show the prize that waits on the sacrifice of a lower end – this *is* reasonable and right. And when men, even angry men, see the right, there is a possibility that they will respond to it.

The issue is complicated by the necessity of the use of force in such ways as police. If a policeman, why not a soldier? Quakers have never been distressed by the police, though they have been distressed by other aspects of compromise, such as the paying of taxes that go to the support of war. The whole issue is too complicated to discuss here, but it is in any case beside the point. Compromise there must always be, and logic must always fail in the attempt to lay down a whole rule of life, though logic could make its stand on the difference in kind, and not merely in degree, between a policeman maintaining order in a healthy community and two power blocs striving their utmost to destroy each other. But even if it be regarded as plain compromise, the pacifist takes his stand at a certain point and says, I can go no farther. Here I draw the line. And the line is drawn always on this side of armed combat, because the kingdom to which he owes allegiance is not of this world, nor to be won by the might of this world. It is possible, in plain human experience, to love a frustrated, deprived child who has become a hooligan by restraining him, confining him, and seeking to cure him; but it is not possible to love a nation by obliterating its cities. The one may tail off imperceptibly into the other, but only by a monstrously long series of gradations; and the line can be drawn broadly but firmly in between.

Here, then, is the constructive message of the pacifist negation, in the belief that there is a capacity in all men for a response to the living truth if we can reveal it by casting aside the armour that covers it. But this generation has seen a new dimension to the art of war with which the Christian hope must learn to deal, in the shape of the new weapons of propaganda and the distortion of truth. There has always been lying, but never before has lying been possible on such a large scale, with the prestige of print and radio and pseudo-scientific literature, never so capable of poisoning truth at the source. We are all dependent on reports and reports of reports, on summaries and 'commentaries' and 'inside stories'; and though they may be presented fairly enough, they are frequently coloured by prejudice and partisanship. The man who to one newspaper staff is the champion of freedom is to another a fanatical revolutionary; a staunch conservative is a hidebound tory; one man's modesty is another's prudery. And when words are thus manipulated deliberately and in the interests of evil, the result might be a colossal deception in which honest men are driven to believe that black is white and white black.

What then? Faced by evil so powerful, that threatens to overwhelm not only our bodies but our minds, the very power to recognize and choose the good, what do we do? Do we not here at last arise and fight this ultimate evil? Even here, the Quaker testimony is the same. If we fight this evil with its own weapons we hand the universe over to its power. There is only one hope, that when the spiritual war is undertaken the 'deepest thing' will not be betrayed, because God will not let it be betrayed. Human judgement is fallible, and because it is fallible an honest man might hesitate in the last analysis: Am I right after all? Is it worth it? But if we have done our best to put our powers of judgement at the service of the living truth, and commit the final issue to God, then of course it is worth it. It is the only thing that is. Jesus had his own experience of the same sort, spanning his life from the trial in the wilderness to the trial in the garden. He too wondered if he was right, if he was sure enough of the path to undertake the burden of that particular choice. 'If it be thy will, let this cup pass from me.' But he was certain that he was there to be used, at whatever cost. 'Nevertheless, not my will but thine be done.' Our final insight into any problem that is going to cost us a great deal to solve will be dim, because the costliness will cloud our vision. But if there is a core of truth in the belief in the inward light of Christ, that dim insight is to be trusted.

The whole complex business of living for love turns back on this choice: Can man know God? If he cannot, then we are at the mercy of our own machinery for justice, our paltry logic, our timidity and prudence, our inability, in the end, to see our way at all. But if he can, then we may devise the machinery itself with a new heart, can follow our logic fearlessly and take up our fears boldly, because we have assurance that the dark ends of our being are in safe keeping. 'Love God and do what you like' is still the heart of the matter, even though you may find yourself driven by your 'liking' to a cross.

In the pursuit of this end, Friends have therefore been uncompromising on the grounds of their action. They have sought to make these grounds positive and constructive by pressing upon negotiating parties – and even more on parties that have ceased to negotiate – the necessity for 'clearness' and integrity in their dealings with one another; and the Quaker tradition of 'advising monarchs' has been largely directed to this end. They have usually been found, two or three of them, or emissaries of a Yearly

Meeting, pressing the claims of truth upon both sides. They are usually present somewhere behind the scenes at meetings of the United Nations. They seek audience of ministers, presidents, kings, dictators. Some Friends with expert knowledge will be found approaching permanent officials, whom they regard as human beings with the same ultimate spiritual responsibility as other men. And all this is not the action of a small pressure-group, seeking to jockey itself into a position of power, but of men speaking to men, raising the issues of love and truth. One such effort was the visit to Moscow in 1951, when a small group of Friends made personal contact with leaders of Russian political, religious and social life, confronting them with plain criticism and seeking to explain the aspects of Western life and thought which caused the Russians anxiety, and endeavouring to reconcile the tension between the two on a basis of truth and respect for human right. This was but one of a long series of visits to Russia, following a visit by two eighteenth century Friends to Czar Alexander I, and including many contacts made through schemes of relief. These small efforts at large things seem trivial, naive and arrogant to those who think only in terms of large, impersonal forces at work through a vast array of officialdom and the 'will of the people'. But the people are persons, and their will is expressed through persons; and persons are the object of God's redemptive care. We cannot measure the power of the universe with our puny scale.

Involved in this reconciling, productive effort is also the well-established Quaker tradition of relief. Here is another of the 'Quaker simplicities', as well known as, and better understood than, the peace testimony. The Friends Ambulance Unit – for which Friends bore a great deal of responsibility, though its membership was immensely wider – worked through two world wars, going into danger as freely as the national armies, accepting a large measure of military direction, but preserving always the right, where geography permits its exercise, to put itself at the service of both sides. Friends Relief Service, more directly a Quaker concern, tended to work more independently of military and political control, and had a wider field of activity, with a stronger bias towards the 'home front', but ranging also over the world, and seeking wherever possible to follow the trail of destruction, and perform the personal rehabilitation and individual care that is so easily neglected by large-scale international relief.

Food, clothes and shelter are all desperately needed when war has rolled across the life of a nation; but when they are supplied, there is still need for understanding, reassurance and the warmth of affection. And though these were often forthcoming from official relief workers, there was usually a special task on this personal level for Friends.

This, then, is the basis of the Quaker testimony against war: the refusal to bear arms, the reconciling power of love that clings to the truth and to the hope of truth, and the meeting of human need wherever it may be found, on either side of the lines of conflict. It is offered by a small community who are ready to bear the misunderstanding that such a reversal of ordinary values must expose them to, in the belief that despite appearances the universe is made to work according to the law of love, provided men will learn to bear the burden of it. Some day, the peoples of the world will say together, We have finished with war; we can endure it no longer. When they are ready to say that – and there are signs that our immense strides in making it unendurably vicious have brought them to the point of it – they will be ready to undertake the suffering of a loving purpose as courageously as they have in the past borne the suffering of fear. War has, we are told, brought out the best in us; and so in a sense it has, because suffering does precisely that. 'I have come to look upon suffering,' said Von Hugel, 'as the purest, perhaps the only quite pure form of action.' But if it is to work as the suffering of Christ worked, it must be accepted, offered, loved through, and not merely endured in stubborn courage. Courage the race has had in plenty. Love in its fullest we have seen in Christ, but for ourselves it is yet to learn.

CHAPTER THIRTEEN

'Primitive Quakerism Revived'

THERE are many signs that the Society of Friends, like indeed, the church at large, is passing through a stage of peculiarly radical development. The whole Christian community has gained in what might be described as 'athletic' capacity since it shed the membership that was based only on habit and respectability. It has gained, too, in honesty of self-scrutiny and in the determination to recover its original, fundamental beliefs, as a result of the challenge of communism, and other less dynamic forms of materialism. And it has gained in a sense of urgency arising from the clear vision of the precipice over which the whole race may plunge itself unless our common purposes are radically changed. These conditions, though they make the human heart quail, are more healthy than the illusion of progress and security which dimmed so much vision during the nineteenth century.

In this situation the Society of Friends has been driven to contrast the explosiveness and clarity of its early days with the quiet traditionalism of the present. An American Friend, Elton Trueblood, puts the challenge thus.

The double mark of the renewal of Primitive Christianity initiated by Fox, was the spiritual high tension on the one hand and the continual outreach on the other. Perhaps these are always the marks of validity when Christian vitality reappears. The inner intensity would have been mere spiritual self-indulgence, if Friends had hugged their experience to themselves, but this they could not do. They preached in churches, they preached at fairs, they preached in prison. Swarthmore was indeed their base, and their place of renewal of strength, but it was primarily a place to go *from* rather than a place in which to *remain*. Friends had no notion of becoming a sect or of developing into a highly respected denomination, with well-managed institutions and pious anniversaries. They sincerely believed that their function was to unite all Christendom by the recovery of Christ in the present tense. Friends were personally humble, but the responsibility was great.

Judged by this standard, contemporary Quakerism is guilty of treason to a great dream. Thousands of modern Friends not only do not think of themselves as missionaries, but are a bit uncomfortable when that word is mentioned. Does it not sound a little pompous, they ask, as though we had a superior message to give? After all, they say, other people have a right to their own opinions. We make a virtue of our dullness and boast discreetly of our policy of spiritual aloofness. Thousands of those who call themselves Quakers not only never quake themselves, but never shake anyone else. The very idea seems somehow undignified or lacking in respectable reserve.[*]

An observer who travelled about among Friends would find the same doubt and questioning in the local meetings. Quakerism once meant something to the whole church. It aroused hostility, but it provoked thought; it was rejected, but it challenged. Where is the hostility and the thought today? Modern Friends are accepted, even respected, but they no longer challenge. Early Quakers could claim, and with a measure of truth, to have experienced 'primitive Christianity revived'. Can modern Friends claim to represent primitive Quakerism revived?

It is plainly not a matter of mere imitation, any more than Fox and his followers imitated early Christianity. The conditions have changed, and the response cannot be repeated. But as Jesus called men to know their God for themselves, so the early Friends called on their generation to return to the source of life. Are we, these modern Friends asked, doing the same thing? We have witnessed to certain truths that *follow* upon the knowledge of God, but what of the knowledge itself? Have we shared *that*?

And when the next question is asked, 'Lord, what shall we do that we may?' there is no clear answer. There is nothing to be gained from lashing oneself into a frenzy of enthusiasm – and modern Friends, even in this new mood, would in any case find that a difficult exercise. The galleon may spread its sails, but it cannot bid the wind to blow; and men cannot by taking thought add an inch to their spiritual stature. They can but return to the life and wait for growth. This always seems a hard saying, particularly to the young, for it is natural, in the light of a great ideal, to long to be up and doing. But hard though it is, there is no alternative. For what is asked of man is not action or sacrifice, but readiness. And the first step towards it is to acknowledge one's unreadiness. The doubt and self-searching which has descended upon the Society bears the promise of new growth. It has arisen not merely from the comparison with early days, but, more significantly, from an increased awareness of the demands

[*]*Friends Face their Fourth Century.*

of the present, and the consciousness that the Society is ill-
equipped to deal with them.

One realization that has come upon the Society with great
force is the need for the Christian witness to be world-wide. It is
not enough to interpret human need in the conditions of western
democracies. The nations of the East have risen to their feet,
and the brotherhood of man must now be seen in a wider
context. In the past, the mere geographical spread of Quakerism
was too narrow to rise to this challenge, but today Friends are to
be met in Africa, India, Japan, Lebanon, Madagascar, Singapore —
indeed, all over the world. They are often engaged in a new kind of
approach to the new nations, seeking not to transplant a western
culture, but to develop new forms of creative community. What was
in the past a mission station is now a community centre, in which
the aspirations of rising nationhood can find their own expression,
and the rich spiritual experience of the east can meet and fuse with
the insight of the west. There has grown up a 'chain of Quaker
embassies' as Carl Heath called it, in the capitals of the world,
and at widely differing points of world tension there may be
found small groups of Quaker men and women striving to create
conditions of understanding.

This widening of frontiers has been matched with a new
awareness – shared with the wider Christian community – of the
immense increase in the area of conflict. What was in the past
a brute struggle for power between nations sharing the same
fundamental outlook on life has now become a war of faiths that
are in radical opposition. The challenge of communism, for long
regarded as a class struggle within the western nations themselves,
has now been intensified by the struggle to dominate Asia and the
world.

The Quaker response to this situation has been twofold. First,
Friends say, let us in the west take to heart the moral challenge
of the communist faith. The Christian church has often been
identified with the privileged nation, race or class, and has failed to
demonstrate that Christianity is at heart the most revolutionary
creed the world has known. The teaching of Jesus renders completely irrelevant differences of wealth and status, and demands
from all his followers a radical search for the worth of all men in
the sight of God. If this element of primitive Christianity were
revived, the western nations would be involved in the same selfless
sharing of resources that marked the church after Pentecost, and

seemed so natural to early Friends. Eastern nations are not to be
won by bribes and counter-bribes, but if the Christian west were
to put its vast resources at the disposal of their brother peoples,
not 'distributing aid' but recognizing, quite simply, the interdependence of all men everywhere, the response of the east would
be immediate.

Such a radical change in outlook seems at present beyond the
reach of the west; and Friends are not so naïve that they think it
will come easily. But this is what, along with millions of other
Christians, they stand for. Their own service is offered in this spirit;
and they trust in the future to bring the mighty challenge home
to those who can meet it.

On another level, the challenge of communism is that of a hostile
power. The Soviet bloc has reasons in its own history for its
suspicion of the west, and for the anxiety and expansiveness in
which that suspicion results. This ominous cloud of mistrust can
be dispersed only slowly, by patience and imagination in all coun-
tries. In the meantime, there is a place for meeting between men
and women bearing no kind of political responsibility, to reach
across the frontiers and explore each other's minds and hearts. In
this belief, Friends continue their historic series of visits to Russia,
and the promotion of visits to the west. It would be simple-minded
to claim that such tenuous threads of contact would hold if open
conflict were to arise, but in the present situation they offer a means
whereby understanding can begin to replace misunderstanding,
and the hostile image of each other that the two sides have clung
to may be slowly replaced by awareness of our common humanity.

The west has hitherto been handicapped in its appeal to the east
by its own ambiguous attitude to coloured peoples. Friends take a
clear stand on this issue. In the words of a report drawn up in
1952:

1. We deny any scientific basis for the myth of racial superiority or
    inferiority.

2. We consider ourselves and all men the children of one loving
    Father, and therefore brothers one with another.

3. We believe in the dignity of the human personality.

4. Accepting as we must individual difference of capacity and of
    intelligence among members of all nations and so-called races, we
    nevertheless recognize that all men deserve equal opportunity to
    develop to the limit of their individual ability.

5. We cannot accept the present racial discrimination as necessary or right, and therefore we feel impelled to take individual and corporate action to eradicate it.

'Individual and corporate action' has involved Friends in a variety of work alongside men of different races, the promotion of inter-racial seminars and conferences, and costly protests against colour prejudice, wherever it may be found. The Quaker effort is small and random, and by itself can be of little avail; but it constitutes a steady current in what is now rapidly becoming a vast flow of the tide of world opinion. Friends do not claim the privilege of solving the vast problems against which they make their effort. The solution lies beyond them. What they do claim, is the duty to face them. In the words of St Chrysostom, 'Do not then because you cannot save the world, neglect and despise a few; nor from your desire for great things keep yourself aloof from small.' And as early Friends testified to social equality, and the logic of events took up the lesson, so they testify to racial equality, and to the brotherhood of the nations.

As the Society thus seeks to apply itself to the problems of world tension, it find itself at the same time more aware of the implications of membership in the whole community of Christian people. It is easy to see why Friends should have withdrawn so notably from the larger Christian tradition, but the early emphasis on a few elements in the Christian experience, designed to recall the whole church to a right sense of values, involved a neglect of the rich variety of experience accumulated in the long tradition. Variety is plainly essential if Christian truth is to make its way among all men – and indeed, if it is to be the whole truth. No man knows the whole, and every man's experience of God will be to some extent private, personal, his own and no other's. This, indeed, was what the early Friends were saying: but in the outcome they neglected, and even attacked, certain aspects of experience because they had not met them for themselves. The truth in the Quaker protest against sacramentalism is not that sacraments cannot be used for God's purposes – which they plainly can – but that the formally recognized sacraments are not the only means by which God works his will. Had this truth been recognized by the church at large, there would have been no need for Quakerism to become a sect at all. But it was not, and Friends in their turn exaggerated their position. But three hundred years have worked on the Society, and Friends have come, somewhat to their own surprise (and partly through the large influx of new members 'by convincement" from other denominations) to a new understanding of the validity of the traditional forms. There is still no tendency to regard them as necessary – and here the Quaker testimony is as urgent as ever – but it is widely realized in the Society that sectarianism brings its own losses, and that Christianity is a richer, fuller thing than it had been thought to be.

Quakers are thus represented at the many conferences and meetings that explore the way to Christian unity. Much of the discussion passes them by, because their answer to questions posed by the other denominations is still often to deny that there is any question: the validity of orders, intercommunion, a statement of belief – to Quakers these problems simply do not exist. But they believe that their position is positive and not merely negative, for the search for agreement on external forms and statements is helped, not hindered, by the existence within the whole church of a community who nurture their spiritual life without them. It helps in two ways: first by helping to turn the attention of Christians to the deep life of which these outward forms are the manifestation; and second by preventing an agreement in mere words, a paper treaty, that does not chime with inward unity. It would not serve the cause of unity if a conference were to produce a common statement which the different sects interpreted differently.

And meanwhile, Friends themselves are being changed and enriched by the wider tradition. They have always insisted that theology followed upon experience, and must never be allowed to escape into an intellectual aridity of its own; and this is right and proper, but it is no excuse for neglecting the theology of experience. And so they have recently declared, in a statement on the Quaker attitude to theology,

> If theology is defined as 'thinking about God' it is a proper activity for Quakers. The Quaker faith is Christian. The root and ground of our experience and therefore of our common belief must be the revelation of God in Christ. God expressed His love historically in Jesus of Nazareth, and eternally through the Spirit of Christ. What Jesus was like in history— in his life, teaching, death and resurrection – God is like in eternity. In Jesus 'the power of God and the wisdom of God' are revealed as fully as possible in a human life. Jesus was love incarnate.

This new orientation, in which the whole of the Society is not yet agreed, must take time to bear fruit, but there is a clear recognition now that 'theology' presents an account of experience wider than one man can embrace, and that the study of it is necessary at the same time to interpret our private experience and to enrich it with the fruits of the experience of others. The focal point of this new development is the life of Woodbrooke, the Quaker college that works together with colleges of other denominations in the study of the faith and its implications in service. Here Quakers who can leave their ordinary work for a few weeks or a term or a year come together to widen and deepen their understanding, and slowly the richer life is beginning to affect the scattered meetings up and down the country.

Kindred to this development is a new sense of the need for intellectual equipment adequate to the needs of this generation. There has always been present in Quakerism, as a weakness to which the democratic principle is particularly liable, a suspicion of learning and theorizing and an emphasis on practical achievement. It has now become clear that nobody can honestly offer a contribution to the solution of modern problems unless he understands the complexity of the problems themselves. Though love be the root of the answer, it is not enough to plead for love without showing what it means in practice; and that, in a highly complex age, must be a highly complex thing. The surgeon's knife becomes a weapon of love only when it is used with knowledge and understanding. And no community can *act* in modern society – and Quakerism is action or it is nothing – without knowledge of the conditions and results of action. Nor can an interpretation of the meaning of life be taken seriously unless it 'speaks to the condition' of modern man. It is not enough to dismiss the various intellectual adventures of our time as irrelevant, and repeat the clichés of the 'gospel message'. For such a grappling with genuine intellectual difficulty, intellects need to be trained and understanding achieved. This training Friends have begun to seek, devising new means, appropriate to modern conditions, of developing the religious education of the adult membership.

There are certain elements of peculiar strength in their position. They have had no creed to tie them to the thought form of an earlier century, or to demand patient explanation to succeeding generations, so they are ready to welcome any new quest for truth as a hope of fresh light. At the same time, they know quite clearly 'where they stand'. Their understanding is based on certain fundamental experiences which cannot be ignored. They are rooted in history but not buried by it. This 'contained flexibility' is peculiarly adapted to the needs of our scientific mood, for there is much that is common to the Quaker and the scientist, the Quaker's religious empiricism being as it were the extension of the scientific method to an additional dimension. The main difference is simply that the Quaker has greater expectations, and believes he finds more.

The same contained flexibility is to be seen in the Quaker attitude to the moral dilemma of our time. Western man has at last, he feels, thrown off the dogmatic morality of his grand-parents. He has not abandoned good feeling to the extent that some critics would assert, but he has claimed his right to make his own rules and conventions. With this, Quaker methods would be in agreement: ultimately, man's inner nature must find its expression for itself. But in the first flush of excitement that this new liberty has brought there has been an invasion of moral relativism which is clearly perilous. The study of morals in a spirit of scientific detachment has revealed such wide varieties of codes and custom that we are driven to ask, Are we not making too much of a fuss about a little misconduct? What we regard as 'wrong' is accepted as 'right' in another culture: may we not take our justification from them in giving ourselves a little licence?

This point of view begs the question, Is it not possible that on a certain issue a whole culture may be wrong? – a question which Quakerism has asked of our own culture on such issues as slavery and war. But apart from that judgement, the Quaker search for an inward apprehension of the will of God for each man reconciles at once the moral relativism of different cultures with the belief in a moral absolute. When a man seeks the will of God within, he is seeking for light on his action *now*, in a concrete situation and a clearly marked cultural environment. It might be a different action in another culture but it would express the same principle. The fact that in India the host dismisses his guests and in England the guests dismiss themselves does not mean there is no such thing as courtesy: but it does mean that each individual must find the right action to express his courteous feeling in the context in which he finds himself. The conventions are the symbols with which he communicates an inward attitude; and the symbols, the language of behaviour may vary, but there will always be a truth to be communicated, that must be found in the depths of the personality.

It is this attention to personal, individual values which gives Quakerism its closest relevance to the condition of modern man. We have found ourselves in the grip of the vast machines we have made with such skill and such pride. The size and complexity of our organization have become such as to daunt the spirit of man, and reduce his life to insignificance. How can one man *count* for anything any more, except to his immediate circle? This sense of personal insignificance and of being cut adrift from the secure circle of men and women we know and love is surely at the root of the monstrous growth of neurosis and psychosomatic illness. There can be no 'cure' for this disease, however skilled we may become in reducing the symptoms. The only cure is a return to the right values, from which the right organization is developed. But right values are not recovered by desiring them, any more than health, whether mental or physical, is won by 'snapping out of it'. If we are becoming a diseased generation we can be cured only by returning to the source of health and life.

And that is to be found in the knowledge that a man does count, even now, in the loving life of the universe. An older generation used to express this discovery in the words, 'And then I knew that Christ died for me.' We find it difficult to use that phraseology now, but the experience is still available, in a discovery that Jesus, speaking with his death of the love of God, speaks direct to each man who listens in accents that are mysteriously meant for him. 'Then,' wrote Fox,

> I heard a voice which said, 'There is one, even Christ Jesus, that can speak to *thy* condition', and, when I heard it, my heart did leap for joy.

And this need to be sought out for ourselves, as persons, is common to us all, and is being more and more recognized by psychologists and students of social problems as fundamental. The present emphasis is upon the vital phase of early infancy, and the 'warm, intimate, and continuous relationship with his mother, in which both find satisfaction and enjoyment', the relationship that 'child psychiatrists and many others now believe to underlie the development of character and of mental health.'* As we proceed from our growing certainty of our diagnosis into the at present doubtful field of cure and restoration we shall begin to hear more of the role of later, adult personal relationships.

*Margery Fry in a preface to Bowlby, *Child Care and the Growth of Love.*

The infant lives by his mother; the man lives by his fellow men; and as the infant does not live by milk alone, so the man asks more of his fellows than food and shelter. The child needs a relationship in which 'both find satisfaction and enjoyment'; and the man needs love, a sense of personal interrelatedness that reaches down to the depths. He must matter as more than a craftsman or an operative or a 'hand' : he must matter as a person.

It is this which lies, in the end, at the heart of the experience of Friends. Bewildered at a time of religious strife, they were driven out, man by man, from the ordinary human fellowship of a common belief and a common attitude, and in their temporary solitude they found themselves loved in their inmost life. Separated for the time from the normal source of love, they found it flowing deeper and surer; and were then enriched by a new upsurge of ordinary human fellowship. They met in the depths, and the surface showed the quality of the meeting. And during the varied phases of Quaker experience in the years that followed, when false turns were taken and mistaken emphasis laid, they clung to this central unity in the deepest life. But now, when the Society has shed almost all its early peculiarities, the life of the meetings up and down the country is still sustained by the same experience and the same fruits. They are mostly small meetings – and it is difficult to see how the Quaker method could be applied to large groups. The members are usually well-known to each other, sometimes striking the visitor as an inward-turning community. But they are all alike in believing that they find their unity in their silent worship, when each man in the solitude of his own heart strikes down to a level of consciousness where he finds he is not alone. Robert Barclay described his discovery of this wordless unity in the secret life, in the *Apology*.

> Not by strength of arguments or by a particular disquisition of each doctrine and convincement of my understanding thereby came I to receive and bear witness of the Truth, but by being secretly reached by the Life. For, when I came into the silent assemblies of God's people, I felt a secret power among them, which touched my heart; and as I gave way unto it I found the evil weakening in me and the good raised up; and so I became thus knit and united unto them, hungering more and more after the increase of this power and life, whereby I might feel myself perfectly redeemed; and indeed this is the surest way to become a Christian; to whom afterwards the knowledge and understanding of principles will not be wanting, but will grow up so much as is needful as the natural fruit of this good root, and such a knowledge will not be barren nor unfruitful.

Two hundred years later, the same note was struck by Caroline Stephen:

On one never-to-be-forgotten Sunday morning (in 1872) I found myself one of a small company of silent worshippers, who were content to sit down together without words, that each one might feel after and draw near to the Divine Presence, unhindered at least, if not helped, by any human utterance. Utterance I knew was free, should the words be given; and, before the meeting was over, a sentence or two were uttered in great simplicity by an old and apparently untaught man, rising in his place amongst the rest of us. I did not pay much attention to the words he spoke, and I have no recollection of their purport. My whole soul was filled with the unutterable peace of the undisturbed opportunity for communion with God, with the sense that at last I had found a place where I might, without the faintest suspicion of insincerity, join with others in simply seeking his presence. To sit down in silence could at least pledge me to nothing; it might open to me (as it did that morning) the very gate of heaven. And, since that day, now more than seventeen years ago, Friends' meetings have indeed been to me the greatest of outward helps to a fuller and fuller entrance into the spirit from which they have sprung; the place of the most soul-subduing, faith-restoring, strengthening and peaceful communion, in feeding upon the bread of life, that I have ever known.*

And now in another century, this is still true of those who find themselves isolated by their own sincerity, whose spiritual search leads to questioning of accepted notions and traditional phrases, and who, worshipping in silence, find themselves at one with other seekers because they are at one in their search and in the loving object of it.

*Quaker Strongholds.

Index